DESIGN & CONSTRUCTION
of the Contract Package Concept

DESIGN & CONSTRUCTION
of the Contract Package Concept

Robert E. Bartz

authorHOUSE®

AuthorHouse™
1663 Liberty Drive
Bloomington, IN 47403
www.authorhouse.com
Phone: 1-800-839-8640

Published by AuthorHouse 03/20/2013

ISBN: 978-1-4817-0139-6 (sc)
ISBN: 978-1-4817-0138-9 (e)

Library of Congress Control Number: 2012924153

Any people depicted in stock imagery provided by Thinkstock are models, and such images are being used for illustrative purposes only.
Certain stock imagery © Thinkstock.

This book is printed on acid-free paper.

Because of the dynamic nature of the Internet, any web addresses or links contained in this book may have changed since publication and may no longer be valid. The views expressed in this work are solely those of the author and do not necessarily reflect the views of the publisher, and the publisher hereby disclaims any responsibility for them.

CONTENTS

PREFACE vii

ACKNOWLEDGEMENTS xi

INTRODUCTION xiii

CHAPTER 1
CONTRACT PACKAGE, FORCE ACCOUNT, AND FASTRACK CONCEPTS 1

CHAPTER 2
CONTRACT FORMAT 14

CHAPTER 3
CHECKLIST/EVALUATION 24

CHAPTER 4
CONTRACT PACKAGES WITH FLOW DIAGRAMS 34

CHAPTER 5
CONTRACT SELECTION 137

CHAPTER 6
SUMMARY/CONCLUSION 166

ABOUT THE AUTHOR 175

PREFACE

The Contract Package Concept demonstrates the manner and method of scoping out an alternate Power Generation Facility with alternate fuel capability. When an owner elects to build this type of facility, his primary function is to select an A/E engineering firm to develop a scope so the Contract Packages can be developed. A good working relationship between the owner and the engineering firm is essential to develop the following:

-Project Management
-Organization/Management Development
-Project Control Services
-Estimating, Budgeting and Cost Control
-Planning and Scheduling
-Material Control
-Inspection
-Purchasing/Procurement/Operational Procedures
-Expediting
-Construction Management
-Construction Planning and Scheduling
-Construction
-Record Drawing
-Manuals
-Environmental Studies and Impact Reports
-Technical and Economic Feasibility Studies
-Site Planning
-Site Selection
-Test Procedures
-Quality Compliance and Assurance
-Contract Formulation, Development, Packaging, Administration
-Construction by Modularization

A/E SELECTION/DETAILED DESIGN

At this stage, construction expertise should be utilized in the following areas:

1. Review and make recommendations from a construction standpoint on proposed A/E scope. Areas to be considered include;
   a. Scope of A/E design vs. contractor design. Should be well defined and require owner approval to deviate from plan.
   b. Review scope of proposed studies to assure that design will be optimized from a construction standpoint. For example, plant arrangement studies,

wind/seismic loading requirements, foundation studies, grounding studies, cable and pipe routing criteria, etc.

c. Review A/E responsibilities and procedures for review of sub vendor design data. How will interface be managed between vendors/contractors?

d. Review A/E quality program. Overall program scope. In Plant QC/QA responsibility.

e. Evaluate A/E expediting responsibility.

f. Review A/E responsibility for design of temporary site facilities, offices, roads, laydown areas, construction utilities, etc.

g. Review A/E modeling capabilities and techniques. Physical vs. computer models. Evaluate costs vs. benefits.

h. Evaluate A/E responsibilities for developing construction contract terms and conditions.

i. Review A/E scope in preparing and bidding construction work packages.

j. Review A/E responsibility for on site inspection, design liaison and construction engineering.

k. Review proposed A/E construction management scope.

l. Review A/E warranties and liabilities for accuracy and timeliness of engi8neering documentation. Also, schedule and cost responsibilities.

m. Review extent of A/E delegation of detailed design to vendors or "furnish and erect" contractors. Verify optimum use of "performance specifications" to insure that efficient designs are obtained with minimal risk to the owner.

2. Review and make recommendations on engineering design documentation as it is being produced. Emphasis should be placed on identifying potential impacts to construction and possible improvements as soon as possible so that maximum benefits can be obtained. Techniques which may be utilized include:

a. Identify and propose alternates for design features requiring excessive jobsite labor or special skills not readily available.

b. Propose ways to simplify design and improve constructability.

c. Identify possible areas of excessive design conservatism or marginal design based on previous experience. Suggest techniques to make the design more efficient and constructible. Examples include obtaining additional information to support design such as soil bearing studies, coordination of structural design between adjacent structures, identifying specific point loadings on structures.

d. Review equipment alternatives for possible differences in erection costs.

e. Review A/E designs for compatibility with local building codes and established cost effective building practices in the area.

DEVELOP PROJECT WORK BREAKDOWN/CONTRACTING APPROACH

This activity is often approached in a haphazard and disjointed fashion totally inconsistent with its true importance. During the A/E selection period, a preliminary concept of the project work breakdown is usually developed by the project participants. Prior to the start of any significant detailed design, the work breakdown should be firmed up and formalized in a written plan with as much detail as possible. The importance of establishing this plan early is that it determines the need dates for all items of engineering documentation required to support the contracting plan. Obviously, the schedule for producing this documentation is dependant on available A/E and owner resources and decision making timetables. The plan emphasizes to all concerned that the importance of meeting these need dates and the potential impacts if they are not met.

The importance of utilizing construction expertise, in both developing the contracting plan and identifying corrective action of problems areas cannot be overemphasized. All too often, it has been observed that good plans will deteriorate rapidly into poor ones if discipline is not exercised by all concerned from the beginning. When schedule problems develop in the design phase, the obvious tendency of the A/E is to propose solutions that take the pressure off these activities while enabling the project completion dates to be met. These type "solutions" might include utilizing more force account (cost-plus) work than originally planned, or breaking down work packages into smaller ones. Both of these approaches allow the additional time necessary to complete the design, however, the true price may be high in terms of higher bids, jobsite inefficiencies, additional CM costs or contractor claims.

Other solutions may be available which reduce impact on the overall plan such as use of overtime or contract employees by the A/E to recover schedule time. Another approach might be to proceed with purchase of long lead time material which would reduce contractor bidding and mobilization time.

Areas to be evaluated in developing the project work breakdown include the following:

1. Consider project budget and schedule need date. Evaluate risks to owner if project not delivered on schedule and within the budget. Identify contracting techniques which could reduce risk such as use of performance bonds, incentives, liquidated damages, etc.
2. Identify contracting plant schedule constraints such as the timetable for selection of major equipment or completion of design in various areas.
3. Identify construction market conditions that may impact the work breakdown such as industry-wide and local contractor backlogs and equipment and material purchase lead times.
4. Evaluate projected inflation rates and impact on proposed contracting methods.
5. Consider management capabilities of the owner/CM organization. What is the size of the CM organization required for the approaches being considered? What activities does the owner want to control directly and what can be delegated to contractors?
6. Identify proposed owner-furnished equipment and services. It may be worthwhile to review established owner policies concerning which items will be purchased directly.
7. Consider the plant arrangement in developing "natural" work limit boundaries for contractors. Look at ways to avoid "stacking" several contractors in a given area.

8. Develop optimal assignments of responsibility for providing insurance (owner "wrap up" program), safety, first aid, security, scheduling/cost reporting, QC/QA construction inspections, construction equipment, office space, warehousing, labor relations, surveying and layout, pre-operational test and startup, etc. Also consider how invoices will be approved and paid and who will be responsible for coding the payments to the owner's accounts.

9. Develop subcontracting policy/guidelines. To what extent will prime contractors be allowed to sub contract work? Identify critical performance areas where the work must be preformed with the prime contractor's own forces.

10. Develop standard terms and conditions consistent with the contracting approach for the various types of contracts to be used on the project.

11. Identify which "unknowns" concerning the project would prevent optimizing the contracting approach. Examples might be unknown site subsurface conditions or lack of a decision on a major equipment purchase. Identify potential "work arounds" that would improve the overall plan.

12. Evaluate labor conditions at the site which might impact the contracting plan. Productivity and availability of the required skills should be considered. What are the benefits of performing additional work offsite? Evaluate options for contracting with union or non-union firms. What are the potential problems with each? Consider desirability of a project labor agreement.

ACKNOWLEDGEMENTS

There are countless individuals who offer support and make valuable contributions to the construction of any project. Without these dedicated and supportive individuals, no project can be successful. To all of those individuals, too countless to mention, but too valuable to forget, I offer my thanks.

I also wish to express my deepest thanks to Ryan Boylan-South, Kathy Clanton and Kelly Cash, who took time from their busy schedules to assist in transferring my materials to the pages of this book. I wish to offer a special thank you to Trisha Bartz. Her specific area of expertise is foreign to me, thus the contribution she made is especially gratifying.

It has taken more than twenty years to develop the format and content for this book. I dedicate the countless hours it has taken to research and compile this information to my family…my children, Kathy, Scott and Mike and most of all, to my wife, Marianne. These pages would not have become a reality without their support, sacrifice and love which allowed me the valuable gift of time to compile this work. I thank them daily for their precious gift which allowed me to do what I love to do. It is my hope that my years of experience in the construction field and my desire to pass on my knowledge and experience to those who have less experience will be of value and service.

INTRODUCTION

The new methodology of building Power Plants over the years has greatly impacted the traditional approach. The Co-generators, Independent Power Producers, Developers and Utility Owners are assuming the responsibility for managing project personnel and ensuring that all construction related activities are properly completed instead of one Prime Contractor, or major A/E Construction Firm.

The past three years have appeared favorable to the Co-generators, Independent Power Producers and Electrical Utilities, such as low interest rates, availability of fuel, etc. They have not been impacted with the trends of the 1980's & 1990's of spiraling construction cost and rising interest rates and inflation and increased fuel cost affects have literally paralyzed the construction of new power plants facilities for the past few years. The needs of the nation now call for more electrical capacity demand. Power Plants were designed for base load operation, but they have been operated as Peaking Units. The wear and tear on these units have been astronomical, these units aged twice as fast because they were not designed to operate in that manner or method. It should be known that 50% of our fossil generating plants are over 50 years old.

The purpose of this book is to explain how the Contract Package Concept came about, explain what factors and guidelines are required in making their decision to manage and construct a Power Generation Facility.

The late 1970's & 1980's was a period of mass construction of Fossil Power Plants, which used variable fuels, such as;

* Oil	* Natural Gas/Oil
* Coal	* Coal/Oil
* Natural Gas	* Diesel
* Gas Turbines	* Waste Refuge
* Wood Waste/Burning	

The majority of these units were in the range of 50MW to 850MW. The shortage of new fossil power plants would result in brown outs, black outs or power shortages. It also became apparent the availability of Transmission Lines was not available and could not wheel power to areas needing electricity.

It was during this period of time that the Nuclear Power Plants made there debuts. In the United States it is estimated that more than 100 Nuclear Plants were constructed at more than 70 different sites in 34 states and operated by more than 50 different companies.

The 1990's brought higher interest rates, increase cost of fuel, and availability of fuel. The Utilities wanted to maintain growth, dependability and quality of their Distribution, that is why they started looking at other options;

      * Life Extension   * Repowering with Combustion Turbines
      * Fuel Cell   * Refuse/Waste & Tires
      * Solar   * Incineration
      * Hydro

It was also the time that Co-generators, Independent Power Producers and Power Brokers stepped forward by providing various Electrical generation facilities for a price. The type of plants were:

      * Combine Cycle &/or Coal Gasification
      * HRSG—Heat Recovery Steam Generation
      * Replication
      * Waste Incineration

The question is can the utilities of today adapt to the fast-track low cost construction mentality that has been characterized by Co-generators, Independent Power Producers, and Power brokers?

The answer to this question is YES! It is being accomplished by strong Utility Project Management Teams that have developed strong Project Controls to monitor the budget, schedule and the quality of any type of power project using the Contract Package Concept.

The utilities in the United States have demonstrated and produced construction cost and management formats that are cost competitive with Co-generators, Independent Power Producers, and Purchase Power Developers. A/E and Construction Firms and Contractors must realize the key issues that Utilities of today have to contend with, are Design, Standardization, Project Size, Type of Project, Cost of Fuel, Location, EPA Standards, and Regulations and most important Customer Satisfaction.

The key issue is constructing a Power Plant on schedule or ahead of schedule, and within the budget or under the budget. This is the tight fisted mentality the Utility must take to be competitive. To accomplish this task, the first thing the Utility must begin with is developing a Pre-Planning Stage which must be an integral part of design, engineering, project contracting, procurement, and the constructability of said project. A/E Constructors will find in today's Utility Corporate Management's commitment starts with providing Prudent Project Management Organization to develop and monitor their Plant so it will be Reliable, Dependable and Maintainable with the highest degree of Quality. The Utility using the Contract Package Concept will be very cost conscious, with a tight fisted mentality that will be carried over to the Utility Project Management Onsite. The purpose of this book, is for A/E and Contractor Firms and Contractors to assist & benefit them for knowledge on just how the Utility works.

CHAPTER 1

CONTRACT PACKAGE, FORCE ACCOUNT, AND FASTRACK CONCEPTS

INTRODUCTION

The fastrack optimum mix concept of contract packages and force account work is not new in the construction of fossil power plants. However, re-examination and application are most important for the successful control of a project's cost and schedule in light of today's continuing inflation and cost escalation.

This book is based upon the following premises:

a. Owner acts as its own prime contractor and construction manager.
b. Engineering design is by an Architect/Engineering firm.
c. A Construction management firm, labor, broker, or contractor can provide force account personnel.
d. Owner's site manager directs an integrated site construction management organization of Owner and Architect Engineer's personnel, and sub-contractors.

Currently, U.S. power plants have a diverse mix of fuels that are in operation:

- ☐ Nuclear
- ☐ Coal
- ☐ Gas
- ☐ Solar
- ☐ Oil
- ☐ Wind
- ☐ Fuel Cell
- ☐ Geothermal
- ☐ Hydro
- ☐ Gas Turbines
- ☐ Hydrogen
- ☐ Coal/Oil
- ☐ Bio Mass
- ☐ Wood
- ☐ Waste
- ☐ Sugar Cane
- ☐ Tires
- ☐ Rice
- ☐ Paint

The Contract Package Concept can be used for any type of project, industrial, commercial, residential and energy project. The Concept can be adapted to fit any size of project and has the versatility using any type of fuel source or special materials.

WHAT TO SUBCONTRACT

In reviewing the project's scope of work, it becomes obvious that many facets of the work should logically be subcontracted. This includes major work of a highly specialized nature that can best be handled by contractors with the in-depth experience and expertise required for such work. Examples are:

- Major Clearing
- Heavy Earthwork
- Major Dewatering
- Dredging
- Pile Driving
- Marine Installations
- Chimneys
- Storage Tanks
- Thermal Insulation
- Paving

Other work items of a specialized nature that are normally subcontracted to others on an economical fixed price basis include:

1. Elevators
2. Sheet Metal Work
3. Plumbing
4. HVAC
5. Automatic Sprinkler Systems
6. Painting
7. Fencing
8. Roofing
9. Plastering
10. Architectural Specialties:
    - Ceramic Tile
    - Floor Covering
    - Acoustical Ceilings
    - Dry Wall
    - Metal Siding
    - Doors, Windows and Glazing

Final Construction Reports of previous projects document that the foregoing 20 items of subcontracted work represents, on the average, 20% of each project's total manhours.

The remaining 80% of construction manhours is chiefly used in the following major areas:

- Structural Concrete
- Structural Steel
- Boiler
- Turbine Generator
- Condenser
- Other Mechanical Equipment
- Piping Systems
- Electrical Equipment and Systems
- Temporary Facilities and Services

It is in the "80% items" that fastrack's optimum melding of subcontract and force account work must be sought to provide maximum control of the project's cost and schedule.

FASTRACKING

The term "fastracking" is used to identify the construction mode where-in construction is started while overall design is relatively incomplete and continues a pace until design and construction are both complete.

This mode is widely used in power plant construction because of engineering design's long duration. Fastracking would not be necessary and force account work could be minimized if a project could be substantially designed before start of construction, and materials and equipment procured with timely delivery dates. Under such ideal conditions, it would be feasible to subcontract the majority of the "80% items" on a firm price basis.

Most power plants of necessity must be built in the fastracking mode in order to:

1. Construct the plant within a reasonable time frame and meet the scheduled date of operation.
2. Optimize manpower leveling and reduce peak manpower labor force requirements
3. Optimize scheduling and use-factor of construction equipment and tools.
4. Smooth the logistic processes of procurement, delivery, receipt, storage and issuance of materials and equipment.
5. Enhance control of project cash flow.

Fastracking, with its early starts, provides the CPM schedule with many built-in positive float cushions to help absorb the impact of unforeseeable delays, revolting developments and Force Majeure.

Fastracking enables the project to get more "miles per gallon" out of the construction effort.

THE PROJECT'S BASIC WORK COMPONENTS

The project's physical work may be divided into the seven basic components listed below in order to better picture the sequence of the components' construction and to appreciate the logic involved in fastracking and allocation of the work between subcontractors and force account.

The basic components are:

1. Temporary Facilities, Maintenance and Services
2. Substructure
3. Concrete Structures
4. Superstructure
5. Mechanical Equipment and Systems
6. Electrical Equipment and Systems
7. Switchyard

The start of construction of temporary facilities, substructure, concrete structures, and superstructure obviously must follow in that order.

The start of installation of the majority of the "guts" of the plant, the mechanical and electrical equipment and systems, must wait until the superstructure framing, decks and enclosures are substantially complete.

ALLOCATION OF WORK BY BASIC COMPONENTS

Temporary Facilities, Maintenance and Services

1. Buildings, Shops and Sheds
2. Power and Lighting
3. Water and Air
4. Industrial Gases
5. Roads and Drainage
6. Sanitary Facilities
7. Scaffolding
8. Construction Equipment Operation and Maintenance
9. Warehousing and Long Term Storage
10. General Clean-Up
11. Surveying and Lay-Out
12. First Aid
13. Security
14. Building Maintenance
15. Unloading of Materials and Equipment Prior to Award of Installation Subcontracts

Erection of large temporary buildings such as the construction office and warehouses should be sub-contracted on a lump sum basis.

Security services should be provided for by subcontract with a qualified guard service agency.

Installation, maintenance, modifications and operation of all other temporary facilities can best be handled by force account due to changing day to day requirements.

Substructure

1. Excavation, Dewatering, Mudmats and Backfill
2. Foundation Mats and Footings
3. Underground Electrical
   Duct Banks
   Grounding
4. Underground Piping
   Circulating Water Lines
   Open Cooling Water Lines
   Fire mains
   Drainage and Sanitary Piping

Although the plant substructure must be constructed first, it can not be designed until the general arrangements of the plant and site have been developed and approved and the structural and equipment weight loadings have been determined.

As the deep foundation mats and circulating water piping design is firmed-up, lesser foundations, manholes, sumps, etc. can be located. As equipment requirements become known, duct banks, grounding, equipment drains and storm sewers can be designed, routed and interfaced.

The foregoing requirements result in construction drawings being released in piece-meal fashion with "holds" on many drawings particularly in interface areas.

The construction process is further complicated by sequencing of operations for excavation, dewatering, cofferdams, backfill and its stringent compaction requirements.

This in turn is complicated by "layered" construction by ascending elevations and construction priorities of the more important substructure areas.

The most feasible way to work around such difficulties is by force account work. It affords the best control of work scheduling and manpower leveling by diverting labor forces from work stopped by a "hold," interface problem or lack of material to a "go" area with material on hand.

This inherent complete flexibility of force account work is lost when the construction mode is separate firm price contracts for the concrete, electrical, piping and compacted backfill components of the substructure work.

Major substructure excavation should be subcontracted on a unit price basis.

The circulating water lines and open cooling water piping should be subcontracted as specialty work that can be readily coordinated with the other underground work.

The primary goal of substructure construction is completion on or ahead of schedule so as to permit the earliest start of boiler steel erection.

Concrete Structures

1. Turbine Pedestal
2. Intake Structure
3. Discharge Structure
4. Equipment Foundations (Fans, Pumps, etc.)

The above concrete structures comprise a major part of force account concrete construction.

The turbine pedestal schedule is relatively fixed as it must fit into the time slot between substructure construction and start of turbine area structural steel erection.

Construction of the intake and discharge structures provides a balance wheel effect for force account manpower leveling as the schedule for these structures may be shifted from early to midway in the project without jeopardizing major milestone dates.

Force account work provides maximum flexibility for working around engineering holds, material delays and interface problems often encountered in major structures.

It facilitates long and short term planning and scheduling, man power leveling and early starts of critical work activities. Its productivity may be readily monitored and controlled through unit manhour reports.

Construction of certain equipment foundations often has to be delayed until late in the schedule so as not to block access of construction equipment to work areas. Force account permits this flexibility.

Superstructure

1. Structural Steel, Platforms, Stairs, Checkered Plate and Handrail
2. Concrete Decks
3. Masonry Walls
4. Control Building
5. Boiler and Turbine Area Lighting
6. Communication Systems
7. Architectural Features
8. Painting

Engineering design of the superstructure is less hectic than for the substructure because of the longer lead time and as a result there are fewer drawing "holds" and material problems.

Erection of the boiler structural steel is a part of the boiler erection contract. Its early erection is all important to the CPM schedule as the boiler installation involves more manhours than any other component of the project.

The boiler erection contract should be supplemented to include the turbine area structural steel as well as erection of the turbine and intake structure gantry cranes. By utilizing the boiler contractor's ironworker crews on a force account basis, the work can be expedited in an economical manner.

Force account work should be employed to ensure early completion of concrete decks, masonry walls, control building, boiler and turbine area lighting, and communication systems.

By so doing, feedwater heaters, pumps, compressors, switchgear, control panels, etc, may be off-loaded onto their foundations thereby minimizing the costs of rehandling and field storage.

Early installation and use of lighting and communication systems is of great benefit to the construction forces, saves on costs of temporary facilities and results in lower electrical forces at peak of the job.

Painting and architectural work should be subcontracted as specialty work with resultant cost savings.

The primary goal of superstructure construction is substantial completion of superstructure framing, decks and enclosures on or ahead of schedule so as to permit the earliest start of mechanical and electrical equipment, piping and hangers, cable tray, conduit and cable by their respective contractors.

Mechanical Equipment and Systems

1. *Boiler and Accessories
2. *Turbine Generator and Accessories
3. *Condenser
4. *Other Mechanical Equipment
5. *Piping Systems
6. *Piping Insulation
7. *Instrumentation
8. *Gantry Cranes
9. *Elevators

Installation of the above mechanical items should in the main be subcontracted as specialty items

Some of the items should be combined under one contract where-in the contractor has demonstrated ability to handle such combinations.

Examples:

1. Boiler and Condenser
2. Piping, Other Mechanical Equipment and Instrumentation

In so doing, both the project and contractor benefit by:

1. Placing all of one craft under one contractor to reduce competition for same craft labor.
2. Better coordination of union relationships and project safety and security programs.
3. Improved manpower leveling.
4. Fewer contract interfaces.
5. Easier work planning and scheduling.

However, if the Architect Engineer has proven and competitive capabilities in certain of the above starred items, it could be both feasible and desirable cost and schedule wise to install one or more of the items with the Architect Engineer's force account labor. This possibility should be given serious consideration in determining the allocation of work between subcontractors and force account.

Electrical Equipment and Systems

1. Transformers
2. ISO Phase Bus
3. Motors
4. Cable Tray & Conduit Above Grade
5. Power/Control Cable & Terminations
6. B-T-G Board and Recorder Boards
7. Switchgear
8. Motor Control Centers
9. Electrical Instrumentation

All of the above electrical installations should be subcontracted to one electrical contactor.

Switchyard

1. Substructure
   Excavation & Backfill
   Foundations & Manholes
   Duct Banks & Precast Cable Trenches
   Grounding
2. Above Grade Electrical Installations
   Steel Structures
   Busses

OCB's & Disconnect Switches
Conduit & Cable
Line Control Panels

A lengthy engineering time is required to design the switchyard's complex matrix of switching, control and protective equipment so as to properly integrate the plant's generation output with the circuitry of outgoing transmission lines and incoming start-up power. This slow process results in design drawings being released for construction in piece-meal fashion over a long period of time with many "holds" in interface areas.

Construction of the switchyard substructure, including earthwork, foundations, manholes, electrical duct banks, precast cable troughs and grounding, can best be facilitated by fastracking, utilizing the same force account labor assigned to the plant substructure work.

This work will ensure the timely completion of substructure work in order to permit the earliest start of above ground work by the electrical contractor.

The above grade electrical installations, if not subcontracted by the Transmission Department, may logically be included with the plant's electrical work.

FACTORS TO CONSIDER: SUBCONTRACTING VERSUS FORCE ACCOUNT WORK

In determining the allocation of work by basic components the following prerequisites, pro's and con's of subcontracting versus force account work, must be considered and evaluated for minimum impact upon the project's cost and schedule.

Subcontracting Prerequisites

1. Substantially Completed Design
    a. Approved Design Drawings
    b. Approved Engineering Specifications
    c. Approved Vendor's Drawings
    d. Approved Bills of Materials

2. Timely Procurement of Materials and Equipment
    a. Realistic Field Need Dates
    b. Purchase Order with Firm Shipping Dates
    c. Adequate Vendors/Manufacturer's Lead Time
    d. Vendor Surveillance and Follow-up
    e. On-time Shipment

3. Approved Builder's List
    a. Minimum of Three Qualified Contractors
    b. Competitively Interested in Bidding
    c. Capable of Directing, Manning and Financing the Work

4. Contractor's Qualifications
   a. Reputation and Integrity
   b. Management and Supervision
   c. Experience and Expertise
   d. Track Record
   e. Financial Stability
   f. Labor Relations
   g. Construction Equipment

5. Definitive, Well Written Contract
   a. Responsibilities of Contractor
   b. Responsibilities of Owner
   c. Performance Specification
   d. General Conditions
   e. Special Conditions
   f. Equitable Commercial Terms

Advantages of Subcontracting

1. Fixed Prices.
2. Correction of installation errors and poor workmanship is for account of Contractor
3. Cost of labor "show-up" time is for Contractor's account.
4. Cost overruns and loss of profit on account of poor bid estimates, low productivity, mismanagement, labor problems, etc.   are borne by the Contractor.
5. Fixed prices simplify project budgeting.
6. Equipment unloading, storage and preservation is by Contactor.
7. Contractor assumes responsibility during installation of materials and equipment turned over to him.
8. Burden of day to day planning, scheduling and work direction is assumed by Contractor.
9. Burden of craft labor procurement and labor relations is responsibility of Contractor.
10. Burden of labor productivity control is assumed by Contractor.
11. Reduced Architect Engineer craft supervision requirements.

Disadvantages of Subcontracting

1. No direct control over Contractor's productivity.
2. No direct control over Contractor's schedule.
3. All cost savings engendered by good planning, scheduling.   P r o c e d u r e s, methods, supervision and productivity on hard money contracts accrue entirely to the Contractor. On a well managed project this can be a substantial amount, particularly if the work was overbid initially.
4. Misunderstandings and changes in scope can result in costly extras, settlements or legal proceedings.

5. Lack of flexibility in planning, scheduling and manpower leveling engenders extra charges in hard money contracts when confronted with material delays, interface problems, engineering holds and design changes.
6. Requirement of substantially complete engineering design delays preparation of contract packages, contract award and start of Contractor's work.   T h i s serves to increase the Contractor's required manpower level by shortening the available time span in which to schedule the work.
7. Valuable staff time is consumed and extensive overhead costs are incurred in the preparation of contract packages and in the bidding, evaluation and awarding of contracts.
8. Changes in scope of hard money contracts are most apt to result in additional costs higher than anticipated.
9. Multiple contracts create multiple work interfaces between contract boundaries and provide greater chance of interface mismatches with resultant increased costs and delays.
10. Overhead and profit mark-up for Contractor's force account work is substantially higher than the Architect Engineer's mark-up for similar work.

Advantages of Force Account Work

1. Provides direct control over labor productivity.
2. Provides direct control of short term and long range planning and scheduling.
3. Permits "fasttrack" start of construction in critical schedule areas as individual drawings are released, thereby eliminating delays of waiting upon substantially complete designs.
4. Provides maximum flexibility for working around engineering holds, material delays and interface problems.
5. All cost savings resulting from good planning, scheduling, procedures, methods, supervision and productivity accrue to the benefit of the project instead of the Contractor.
6. Saves valuable staff time and extensive overhead costs required for the preparation of contract packages and the bidding, evaluation and award of contracts.
7. Reduces cost and enhances flow of engineering design concepts and drawings through elimination of engineered contract packages and contract drawings.
8. Eliminates claims from contractors for interface problems, late equipment deliveries, schedule changes, engineering holds, etc.
9. Enhances control of cash flow and construction physical progress through direct control of manpower levels.
10. Overhead and profit mark-up for the Architect Engineer's force account work is substantially lower than the Contractor's mark-up for similar force account work.

Disadvantages of Force Account Work

1. No fixed prices
2. Cost of correcting installation errors and poor workmanship is for the account of the project.

3. Cost of labor show-up time is for the account of the project.
4. Cost overruns on account of poor productivity, labor problems, etc.   is borne by the project.
5. Requires additional craft supervisors and a larger non-manual support staff.
6. Increased overheads for tools and supplies normally furnished by the contractors.
7. Lack of profit incentives in controlling costs and meeting schedules.

Potential Benefits: Decreased Number of Contracts

By reducing the number of contracts through incorporation of all work of the same discipline(s) into one major contract for that discipline (i.e. all electrical work handled by one electrical contractor; all boilermaker work and structural steel erection under one boiler erection contractor, etc.) the project's cost and schedule would benefit from:

1. Lower cumulative total of built-in profits and overhead allowances of contracts.
2. Reduced exposure to additional costs from changes in scope of multiple contracts.
3. Reduced frequency and associated costs of interface problems created by contract boundaries.
4. Lower construction management costs through administration of fewer major contracts.
5. Improved manpower leveling for the individual contractors and the overall Project by reducing Contractor's competition for the same craft labor.
6. Improved monitoring of Contractor's efforts by concentrating on fewer contractors.
7. Improved scheduling and higher use-factor of construction equipment.

Contractual Considerations

In subcontracting portions of the project's work, the following guidelines should be considered:

1. Prime contract(s): provide monetary incentives to reduce manhours and/or improve schedule.
2. Contract packages: to be prepared by the Site Manager incorporating the Architect Engineer's engineering specifications and design drawings and vendor's drawings when applicable. Special contract package drawings are not to be prepared by the Architect Engineer.
3. Provide a preprinted "brief form" subcontract format for use by the Site Manager for minor work of short duration not to exceed $20,000.00
4. Minimize number of contract packages to improve control of manpower, planning and scheduling and management of the work.
5. Wherever feasible, base contracts upon unit prices, or a series of lump sums, rather than one lump sum.
6. All contracts: include an equitable pricing basis for performance of force account work.

SUMMARY AND RECOMMENDATIONS

The foregoing discussion has hopefully identified and presented the logic for:

A. The necessity for and advantages of employing the fastrack construction mode in power plant construction.

B. The twenty items of work that should logically be subcontracted on all projects.

C. The "80% items" of construction work as the area of concern regarding subcontracting versus force account implementation.

D. The projects seven basic work components and their construction sequence.

E. The allocation of work (subcontract or force account) of the project's basic work components.

F. Prerequisites for subcontracting, advantages and disadvantages of subcontracting and force account work, potential benefits from limiting the number of subcontracts and important considerations concerning the design of contracts.

In due consideration of the above, it is recommended that:

A. In order to best control the project's cost and schedule that the Owner act as its own prime contractor and construction manager with the Owner's Site Manager directing the integrated site construction management organization composed of Owner's and Architect Engineer's personnel.

B. The fastrack construction mode be employed from the start of construction in order to best meet the scheduled date of operation.

C. Subcontracting be employed for the twenty items of work logically subcontracted by all projects.

D. Fastract force account mode be employed for:
   1. The Power Plant Substructure.
   2. The Switchyard Substructure.
   3. Concrete Structures (Turbine Pedestal, Intake and Discharge Structure, Equipment Foundations)
   4. Superstructure Framing, Decks, and Enclosures.
   5. Temporary Facilities and Services.

E. Subcontractors be employed for installation of:
   1. Mechanical Equipment and Systems.
   2. Electrical Equipment and Systems.
   3. Switchyard Above Grade Components.

The above allocation of work is based upon the best possible mix to optimize manpower leveling, facilitate scheduling, minimize work interface problems, promote efficient use of manpower and equipment, reduce overhead costs and enhance direction and control of the total Project.

CHAPTER 2

CONTRACT FORMAT

The previous chapters of this book have been developed to help explain and clarify the various manner and methods in which will help explain how an owner can and might use the Project Management concept for any size or type of projects

Project size, complexity durations and geographic location may have a major influence on the choice of the contract package concept method for construction. The primary motivation for use of the Contract Package Concept is to break the job into proper and efficient size packages which can be bid and awarded on a "lump sum basis."

In general, fixed price contracts should not follow or be dependent upon work which is subject to delays and uncertainties, as such conditions will tend to void the original contract terms. For any specific job it would be possible, by analysis of the risk to the owner, to determine which contract concept work would be contracted and which should be done by force account.

It is necessary to have engineering and design complete at an early date on construction contract if the benefits of lump sum contracts are to be realized. This is necessary to award the contracts in as large contracts as possible and in a timely manner.

In developing the format for Contract Package Concept starts with dividing types of work to be completed in a scheduled format. Once plotted on paper with the basis format established, the owner then can add or delete or rotate types of work. Once it is identified what type of project that will be built, the owner will develop a tentative list of contract packages which an owner may anticipate would be used to build the project. Enclosed is a suggested list of contracts for building a power plant. It helps the owner evaluate the status of engineering, procurement, etc. which in turn allows the owner to finalize how the segments of the project will be built by Force Account or Contract Packages.

In developing the format for the Contract Package Concept starts with developing the types of work to be completed in a schedule format (Figures 1, 2, 3 &4).

BASIC CONSTRUCTION
FOSSIL POWER PLANT
SCHEDULE

SCOPE DEFINITION

    INCLUDES A LISTING OF ITEMS & SERVICES THAT

    OWNERS / AE FIRM / CONTRACTORS PRIM CONTRACTOR WILL PROVIDE

PROJECT ORANIZATION

    TYPE OF ORGANIZATION

    LIST SUITED MEET PROJECT

    NEEDS / LIST SPECIFIC RESPONSIBILITIES

PROJECT DEVELOPMENT PLAN

    A WRITTEN DOCUMENT THAT   IDENTIFIES WHAT, WHEN,

    WHO, HOW MUCH, HOW OFTEN & WHY

INTEGRATED PLANNING SCHEDULE

    MAJOR MILESTONES FOR   LICENSING / PERMIT

    ENGINEERING

    PROCUREMENT

    CONSTRUCTION

PERMIT / LICENSING ACTIVITIES

SITE EVALUATION

    AGREAGE   TRANSPORTATION LIMITATIONS

    WATER AVAILABILITY   LAND USAGE

    ELECTRICAL AVAILABILITY   LAY DOWN AREA

    DISTANCE CONSTRAINTS   DE-WATERING

    ENVIRONMENTAL FACTORS

PRE DESIGN / CONSTRUCTON PLANNING

SITE PLANNING FOR TEMPORARY FACILITIES

    UTILITIES   BUILDINGS

    – ELECTRICITY   – CONST. OFFICE

    – WATER   – FAB SHOP – ONSITE

    – SEWAGE   – WAREHOUSE

        – LAY DOWN AREA

        – ACCESS ROADS / RIVER DELIVERY

FIGURE #1

DESIGN / CONSTRUCTION COORDINATION

- INTEGRATED PROJECT SCHEDULE
- CONSTRUCTION SEQUENCING
- IDENTIFICATION OF MILESTONES
- PROCUREMENT / FABRICATION SCHEDULING
- SITE PLANNING FOR TEMPORARY FACILITIES
- CONSTRUCTABILITY REVIEW OF DRAWINGS & SPECIFICATIONS
- PROJECT COORDINATION

PLANNING FOR FIELD MOBILIZATION

- CONSTRUCTION PROJECT ORGANIZATION
- PRE CONSTRUCTION LABOR REVIEW
- PREPARATION OF SITE LAYOUT

FILED MANAGEMENT

- CONSTRUCTION MANAGEMENT
- FIELD MANAGEMENT APPLICATON OF BASIC MANAGEMENT TECHNIQUES OF COORDINATION MONITORIN EVALUATION AND DOCUMENTATION TO ACHIEVE CONTRACTOR CONTROL.

ORGANIZATION

- FIELD CONSTRUCTION MANAGEMENT
- FIELD ENGINEERING
- CONTRACTOR CONTROL
- PROJECT ADMINISTRATION
- QUALITY CONTROL

CONTRACTOR CONTROL FUNCTIONS

- CORRESPONDENCE
- MEETINGS
- FILE / INFORMATION SYSTEMS
- CONTRACT INTERPRETATION
- OWNER / CONTRACTOR CONTRACT

DOCUMENTATION OF PERFORMANCE

FIGURE #2

CONTRACTOR CONTROL REQUIREMENTS

- PRE-CONSTRUCTION PLANNING AND THOROUGH KNOWLEDGE OF EACH CONTRACT
- CLEAR UNDERSTANDING OF WORK RULES
- ADEQUATE REPORTING
- CONFORMANCE WITH DRAWINGS & SPECIFICATIONS
- PROGRESS & CONTROL EVALUATIONS
- EFFECTIVE CLOSEOUT PROCEDURES
- PERFORMANCE APPRAISALS

FIELD MANAGEMENT SUPPORT SERVICES

- CONSTRUCTION ACCOUNTING
- MATERIAL CONTROL / FIELD PURCHASING
- SYSTEMS SUPPORT
- PLANNING & SCHEDULING
- BUDGET / ESTIMATE
- APPROVED PROJECT ESTIMATE
- COST ENGINEERING

  CODING

  CASH FLOW FORECASTS

  MANPOWER

  QUANTITIES

  COMPLETION CURVES

LABOR COORDINATION

SAFETY

SECURITY

START-UP / FINAL PUNCHLIST CLOSING OUT PROJECT

FIGURE #3

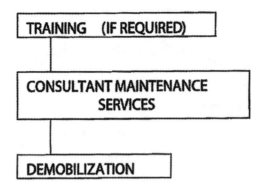

FIGURE #4

Once plotted on paper with the basic construction schedule established by the owner, then the owner can add or delete or rotate types of work.

A suggested draft of the work activities, necessary to meet the project milestone, will be addressed later in this Chapter.

CONTRACT PACKAGE—LISTING SUGGESTED METHOD OF CONSTRUCTION

Site Preparation—Force Account
Work to include:

1. Construction of access roads, preparation of railroad subbases, laydown areas, drainage ditches, temporary small building and construction air and water lines. Large building, if any, to be sub-contracted.
2. Installation of construction power facilities including substations, distribution centers, underground duct runs and electrical connections to temporary facilities and yard lighting.

Circulating Water and Cooling Water Lines—Contract/Force Account
Work to include:

1. Installation of circulating water lines and testing of same.
2. Installation of underground open water lines and testing of same.

Substructure Construction—Force Account/Contract
Work to include:

1. Excavation, dewatering (as required), mudmats, and backfill for all building and structure foundations, Force Account.
2. Form, install reinforcing steel, embedded steel, plumbing and electrical work, and concrete for all building and/or structural foundation mats, footings and grade beams including manholes, vaults and sumps. (Boiler foundations, turbine and generator, precipitator and stack foundation could be done by specialty contract, Engineering permitting.)
3. All underground electrical duct banks and grounding.
4. All underground piping including fire mains, drainage and sanitary piping, but excluding circulation water and open cooling water lines.

Concrete Structures, Equipment Foundations and Masonry—Force Account
Work to include:

1. Form, install reinforcing steel, embedded steel, electrical work, and concrete for intake structure, discharge structure, turbine pedestal, equipment foundations, concrete floor slabs and decks, and concrete tie-beams and columns.

2. Erect masonry walls and partitions including incorporated doors, windows, louvers, ceilings, special floors, etc.
3. Erect all miscellaneous steel in connection with above.

Boiler, Condenser, Structural Steel and Gantry Cranes—Contract

Work to include:

1. Erection of all boiler components furnished by boiler vendor including fans, air preheaters, air and gas ducts, boiler modules and steam drum erection. Excludes coal handling system, precipitator and ductwork and SO2 removal equipement.
2. Erection and tubing of condensers.
3. Erection of boiler structural steel and turbine area structural steel.
4. Erection of turbine and intake gantry cranes.

Early Scheduled Electrical Installations—Force Account

Work to include:

1. All station lighting in the boiler, turbine plant and yard areas.
2. Communications systems.
3. Structural steel grounding
4. Welding systems.
5. Power to turbine and intake gantry cranes.
6. Major cable tray runs.

Plant Electrical Installation—Contract

Work to include:

1. Installation of all above ground conduit, grounding, balance of cable tray, pull boxes, terminal boxes, remote mounted push-buttons and major starters.
2. Install and connect Owner furnished electrical equipment including power transformers, isolated phase bus and accessories, turbine-generator plant electrical accessories including excitation cubicle, water and waste treatment electrical accessories, boiler plant electrical accessories, auxiliary electrical accessories, motors, emergency generator, metal clad switchgear, buses, power centers, vital ac/dc system equipments, motor starters, batteries and chargers, motor control centers, terminal cabinets, relay cabinets, cathodic protection system and power/control cable.
3. Pull, ring out, test and connect all power and control cable.
4. Provide craft labor to assist in final testing, calibration and startup as directed by the Owner.

Power Piping and Installation—Contract

Work to include:

1. Furnish, install and test all power piping systems, including hangers, supports and restraints for mainstream, hot and cold reheat, extraction steam, auxiliary system,

boiler feed, condensate, air evacuation, closed cooling water and miscellaneous drips, vents and drains, including hangers, hanger support steel, restraints, valves (as required) and specialties.

2. Install all Owner furnished valves and specialties.
3. Install balance of plant piping furnished by Owner. Excludes piping furnished with boiler and turbine-generator.
4. Flushing of condensate/boiler feed piping and blowing out of mainstream and reheat piping.
5. Provide craft labor to assist in final testing, calibration and start-up activities as requested by Owner.

Mechanical Equipment Installation—Contract

Work to include:

1. Erect, align and balance turbine generator and accessories; all pumps, compressors, water treatment plant, waste treatment equipment, shop fabricated tanks and miscellaneous mechanical equipment.
2. Provide craft labor to assist in final testing, calibration and start-up activities as directed by Owner.

Instrumentation Installation—Contract

Work to include:

1. Furnish and install all instrument tubing, piping, valves and freeze protection insulation.
2. Install BTG and auxiliary control boards (other than coal handling and electrical systems), computer, and install and calibrate all Owner furnished pneumatic and electronic instrumentation, specialties, gauges, thermometers, etc., except those specifically covered in other contracts.
3. Install all instrument racks and connect
4. Pull, terminate, ring out, and test all instrument and thermocouple wiring. Furnish and install all conduit from trays to devices as required.
5. Provide craft labor to assist in final testing, calibration and start-up as directed by the Owner.

Oil Handling System—Contract

1. Furnish and install entire oil handling system—architectural, structural, electrical, mechanical, elevators, etc. on Owner's foundations.

Precipitator and Ductwork—Contract (Not required if Furnished by Boiler Vendor)

1. Furnish and erect precipitators, all ductwork from air preheater to ID Fans and structural steel support on Owner's foundations; all electrical equipment and connections; hopper heating; bridges, stairs, platforms; electrical equipment room; insulation, etc.

SO2 Removal Equipment—Contract

1. Design, furnish and erect SO2 removal equipment on Owner's foundation. Scope includes structural, electrical, piping, etc., plus all related material handling systems, including ductwork from ID Fans to stack.

SO2 Sludge Removal System—Contract

1. Design, furnish and install SO2 sludge removal on Owner's foundations. Scope includes structural, electrical, piping, etc., plus all related material systems, from thickener underflow to disposal area.

Switchyard Installation—Contract

1. Install switchyard in its entirety, including foundations, control house, structures, buses, equipment, controls, conduit, cable and groundings.

Insulation—Contract

1. Furnish and install insulation on piping, boiler and turbine.

Chimney—Contract

1. Furnish and erect concrete chimney including liner, insulation, platforms, ladders, embedded steel, and all plumbing work.

Field Fabricated Tanks—Contract

1. Furnish, install and paint all field fabricated tanks.

Railroad Siding—Contract

1. Furnish and install rails, switches, ballast, ties, etc., on base prepared by others.

Transformers Fire Protection Sprinkler System—Contract

1. Furnish and install deluge sprinkler systems on main power, aux power and start-up transformers.

Station Painting—Contract

1. Furnish materials and paint all plant structures and equipment except those items included in other contracts.

Boiler Chemical Cleaning—Contract

1. Provide labor, chemicals and equipment to chemically clean the boiler internals.

Roads and Parking Areas—Contract

1. Construct and pave permanent roads and parking areas.

Fencing—Contract

1. Furnish and install all permanent fencing.

In addition to the above there are a considerable number of responsibilities and miscellaneous work items that can best be handled by force account. Such items include:

1. Surveying services
2. Nurse and first aid personnel.
3. Operators for railroad locomotive
4. Unloading of materials and equipment received prior to award of contract for their installation.
5. Long term storage protection of materials and equipment stored outdoors.
6. General clean-up of construction areas.
7. Operate, modify and maintain as required, gas and water systems, compressed air systems, water treatment systems, construction sanitary sewage treatment facilities, welding, lighting and temporary power system.
8. Supply trash containers for trash chutes located in buildings under construction and throughout jobsite and provide for emptying, removal and replacement as required.
9. Provide messenger service for miscellaneous on and off-site deliveries and pickup as required.
10. Perform preventative maintenance and repairs on Owner-furnished construction equipment. Maintain up-to-date records of same.
11. Provide all general services for maintenance, repair and clean-up of temporary buildings.
12. Maintain construction roads, ramps, fencing, parking areas and access walkways.
13. Provide miscellaneous carpentry work, moving of office equipment, furniture, partitions, etc.
14. Provide qualified drivers as required on an as-called basis for site emergency vehicle.
15. Final clean-up and removal of temporary facilities.

CHAPTER 3

CHECKLIST/EVALUATION

Owner participation must start with a set of goals, requirements, priorities and criteria. It is then that the contribution expected of each functional area can be determined and assigned. The enclosed checklist can assist this task.

PRECONSTRUCTION PLANNING

Planning is a KEY to successful project management. In the past, the early stages of a project have not had the opportunity for adequate input. To ensure project success in today's environment, total project planning is important from the start.

It's recommended that the Owners participate in detail in all significant project activities. Depending on circumstances, our participation may involve monitoring, reviewing, advising, approving or directing and implementing activities.

There is no "cookbook" approach to managing the many interrelated activities required to construct a large power plant. The activities listed here are intended to suggest to the prudent owner the areas he should be prepared to look at and provide intelligent input into.

For convenience, pre-construction planning activities can be classified based on which of the following major project activities is being supported:

1. Conceptual Design/Site Selection/Permitting.
2. Architectural Engineer Selection/Detailed Design
3. Develop Project Work Breakdown/Construction Approach
4. Issue Construction/Procurement Contracts.

CONCEPTUAL DESIGN/SITE SELECTION/PERMITTING

Even at the initial stages of a project, construction participation is important in providing input such as the following:

- Evaluate site access considerations. Consider opportunities for modular construction and prefabrication
- Recommend/review subsurface investigation program. Consider risks versus costs in recommending extent of program. Evaluate dewatering considerations.
- Review permitting documents for special environmental protection requirements that will impact construction. Suggest techniques and alternative to reduce costs.
- Evaluate comparative site development costs for proposed sites.

- Review conceptual design documents, facility descriptions, estimates, and schedules for construction considerations.
- Evaluate labor considerations proposed sites.

ARCHITECTURAL ENGINEER SELECTION/DETAILED DESIGN

At this stage, construction expertise should be utilized in the following areas:

1. Review and make recommendations from a construction standpoint on proposed Architectural Engineer scope. Areas to be considered include:
   a. Scope of Architectural Engineer design versus contractor design. Should be well-defined and require Owner approval to deviate from plan.
   b. Review scope of proposed studies to assure that design will be optimized from a construction standpoint. For example, plant arrangement studies, wind/seismic loading requirements, foundation studies, grounding studies, cable and pipe routing criteria, etc.
   c. Review Architectural Engineer responsibilities and procedures for review of subvendor design data. How will interface be managed between vendors/contractors?
   d. Review Architectural Engineer quality program. Overall program scope. In-plant QC/QA responsibility.
   e. Evaluate Architectural Engineer expediting responsibility.
   f. Review Architectural Engineer responsibility for design of temporary site facilities, offices, roads, laydown areas, construction utilities, etc.
   g. Review Architectural Engineer modeling capabilities and techniques. Physical versus computer models. Evaluate costs versus benefits.
   h. Evaluate Architectural Engineer responsibilities for developing construction contract terms and conditions.
   i. Review Architectural Engineer scope in preparing and bidding construction work packages.
   j. Review Architectural Engineer responsibility for on-site inspection, design liaison and construction engineering.
   k. Review proposed Architectural Engineer construction management scope.
   l. Review Architectural Engineer warranties and liabilities for accuracy and timeliness of engineering documentation. Also, schedule and cost responsibilities.
   m. Review extent of Architectural Engineer delegation of detailed design to vendors or "furnish and erect" contractors. Verify optimum use of "performance specifications" to ensure that efficient designs are obtained with minimal risk to the Owner.

2. Review and make recommendations on engineering design documentation as it is being produced. Emphasis should be placed on identifying potential impacts to construction and possible improvements as soon as possible so that maximization benefits can be obtained. Techniques which may be utilized include:

25

1. Identify and propose alternates for design features requiring excessive jobsite labor or special skills not readily available.
2. Propose ways to simplify design and improve constructability.
3. Identify possible areas of excessive design conservatism or marginal design based on previous experience. Suggest techniques to make the design more efficient and constructible. Examples include obtaining additional information to support design such as soil bearing studies, coordination of structural design between adjacent structures, identifying specific point loading on structures.
4. Review equipment alternatives for possible differences in erection costs.
5. Review Architectural Engineer designs for compatibility with local building codes, and established cost effective building practices in the area.

DEVELOP PROJECT WORK BREAKDOWN/CONTRACTING APPROACH

This activity is often approached in a haphazard and disjointed fashion totally inconsistent with its true importance. During the Architectural Engineer selection period, a preliminary concept of the project work breakdown is usually developed by the project participants prior to the start of any significant detailed design, the work breakdown should be firmed up and formalized in a written plan with as much detail as possible.

The importance of establishing this plan early is that it determines the need dates for all items of engineering documentation required to support the contracting plan. Obviously, the schedule for producing this documentation is dependant on available Architectural Engineer and owner resources and decision making timetables. The plan emphasizes to all concerned the importance of meeting these need dates and the potential impacts if they are not met.

The importance of utilizing construction expertise in both developing the contracting plan and identifying corrective action if problems arise cannot be overemphasized All too often, it has been observed that good plans will deteriorate rapidly into poor ones if discipline is not exercised by all concerned from the beginning. When schedule problems develop in the design phase the obvious tendency of the Architectural Engineer's to propose solutions that take the pressure off these activities while enabling the project completion dates to be met. These type "solutions" might include utilizing more force-account (cost-plus) work than originally planned, or breaking down work packages into smaller ones. Both of these approaches allow the additional time necessary to complete the design, however, the true price may be high in terms of higher bids, jobsite inefficiencies, additional CM costs or contractor claims.

Other solutions may be available which reduce impact on the overall plan such as use of overtime or contract employees by the Architectural Engineer to recover schedule time. Another approach might be to proceed with purchase of long lead time material which would reduce contractor bidding and mobilization time.

Areas to be evaluated in developing the project work breakdown include the following:

1. Consider project budget and scheduled need date. Evaluate risks to owner if project not delivered on schedule and within budget, identify contracting techniques which could reduce risk such as use of performance bonds, incentives, liquidated damages, etc.

2. Identify contracting plan schedule constraints such as the timetable for selection of major equipment or completion of design in various areas.

3. Identify construction market conditions that may impact the work breakdown such as industry-wide and local contractor backlogs and equipment and material purchase lead times.

4. Evaluate projected inflation rates and impact on proposed contracting methods.

5. Consider management capabilities of the Owner/CM organization. What is the size of the CM organization required for the approaches being considered? What activities does the owner want to <u>control</u> directly and what can be delegated to Contractors?

6. Identify proposed owner-furnished equipment and services. It may be worthwhile to review established owner policies concerning which items will be purchased directly.

7. Consider the plant arrangement in developing "natural" work limit boundaries for contractors. Look at ways to avoid "stacking" several Contractors in a given area.

8. Develop optimal assignments of responsibility for providing insurance (owner "wrap up" program), safety, first aid, security, scheduling/cost reporting, QC/QA construction inspections, construction equipment, office space, warehousing, labor relations, surveying and layout, preoperational test and startup, etc. Also consider how invoices will be approved and paid and who will be responsible for coding payments to the Owner's accounts.

9. Develop subcontracting policy/guidelines. To what extent will prime contractors be allowed to subcontract work? Identify critical performance areas where the work must be performed with the prime contractor's own forces.

10. Develop standard terms and conditions consistent with the contracting approach for the various types of contracts to be used on the project.

11. Identify which "unknowns" concerning the project would prevent optimizing the contracting approach. Examples might be unknown site subsurface condition or lack of a decision on a major equipment purchase. Identify potential "work arounds" that would improve the overall plan.

12. Evaluate labor conditions at the site which might impact the contracting plan. Productivity and availability of the required skills should be considered. What are the benefits of performing additional work offsite? Evaluate options for contracting with union or non-union firms. What are the potential problems with each? Consider desirability of a project labor agreement.

ISSUE CONSTRUCTION/PROCUREMENT CONTRACTS

Once the contracting approach has been determined, it is important that the Owner maintain detailed oversight of the necessary construction contracts to assure that the plan is being followed. Many options, potential deviations and critical decisions will present themselves during this phase which will again require that a high degree of construction expertise be available.

Activities to be reviewed include the following:

1. Verify that the overall approach of the contract package is consistent with the project approach. Check scope, method of bidding, etc.
2. Verify consistency between contract special and general conditions.
3. Verify that drawings and specifications are complete for the defined scope of work. Check that scope is clearly marked on drawings and is consistent with written documents.
4. Conduct final detailed review of drawings from a constructability standpoint to identify remaining problems.
5. Review bid forms for consistency with project scope and required level of detail. Are unit prices required for potential changes? Are labor and material markups being quoted? Inefficiency rates for extended work hours or shift work? Equipment rates?
6. Review bid document addenda as they are issued.
7. Review instructions to bidders for clarity and completeness.
8. Review planned bid evaluation method for fairness and consistency with project requirements. What options, unit prices will be evaluated?
9. Assure that the schedule incorporated in the contract interfaces accurately with the overall project schedule. Incorporate detailed system/equipment need dates in accordance with the owner's startup schedule as appropriate.
10.
11. Assist in preparation of contractor bid lists. Evaluate contractors for experience and capability to bid on individual contracts.
12. Assist in evaluation of bids. Discuss clarification and exceptions with bidders as appropriate. Assure that bids are properly weighted to indicate the trust costs to the Owner for equivalent services.

CHECKLIST-EVALUATION OF TECHNICAL PROPOSAL

1. Is there a clear concise statement of the technical requirements which the proposal fulfills or in the case of an unsolicited proposal, the particular areas involved?
2. Is the technical problem as seen by the customer clearly delineated? Not simply "parroted" from Request for Proposal? Is the proposal responsive to the technical requirement?
3. Does the proposal convincingly show a depth of understanding of the problem?
4. Is there a brief discussion of alternate solutions which were explored and rejected and the reason for their rejections?

5. Is there a discussion of technical approaches to be explored and why the company's approach may be expected to yield the desired results?
6. Is the proposal responsive to all the tasks required by the Request for Proposal?
7. Does the proposal indicate clearly the approach to accomplishing all requirements?
8. Have all "special" requirements in the Request for Proposal been included?
9. Does the proposal respond to the Request for Proposal requirements without unnecessary additional or different problems?
10. If the proposal contemplates more effort than requested in the Request for Proposal, has the additional effort been justified on the bases that is technically and economically desirable?
11. Does the proposal commit the company to requirements that can be accomplished, or are there potential cost of technical problem areas?
12. If the proposal is an unsolicited one, is it based on the customer's needs and desires or what the company wishes to sell?
13. Have unrealistic and unreasonable performance requirements been identified and alternatives suggested?
14. In the event of deviations or alternates, is the detail logic for these recommendations given? Especially in terms of benefits, such as enhanced performance, lower costs, greater producibility, earlier delivery and simpler main tenance.
15. In the event that certain problem objectives are to some extent incompatible with other problem goals (e.g. simplicity versus accuracy) does the proposal unequivocally show that the optimum solution, all factors considered, has been attained?
16. Have the more difficult areas been identified and detailed provided showing how performance requirements never before achieved will be met?
17. Have excessive costs or time delays required to meet certain specific requirements been clearly pointed out?
18. If originality has been spelled out as a requirement, does the proposal represent a unique imaginative approach?
19. Is there a description of novel ideas of technical approaches?
20. Is there a statement of major technical problems which must be solved with an indication as to the amount of effort budgeted to each?
21. Is the relation of proposed solution to the broader over-all system with which it will operate shown?
22. Is there a description of the hardware which the contractor expects to furnish?
23. Is there a conservative estimate of the item's performance?

CHECKLIST-EVALUATION OF A MANAGEMENT PROPOSAL

1. Does the proposal clearly demonstrate an understanding of the customer's concern with the management of this project?
2. Are details provided on corporate experience, facilities and personnel?
3. Does the proposal demonstrate that top-level management will continue a high level of interest and assume responsibility for successful accomplishment of the program?

4. Does the proposal provide convincing evidence that the company is properly oriented and organizationally structured to meet the specific management needs of this project? Especially in terms of providing the requisite functions of communication (internal and external) and of integration of all project phases and pieces?

5. Is evidence given of management's understanding of how the specific project, fits into the customer's over-all needs?

6. Does the proposal indicate that management first has taken a completely objective and detached look at the entire problem prior to thinking in terms of specific solutions?

7. Is it clear that management has honestly examined its own areas of competence and incompetence?

8. Are details provided on management objectives, policies, participation and reliability concepts?

9. Does the proposal show the capabilities of the management to handle a project of the size contemplated?

10. Is evidence given that top-level management has full control of its organization?

11. Does the proposal show how the interest of the company in this specific project ties in with the company's long-range plans as well as with past experience?

12. Does the proposal outline the type of management to be provided for the project, via; whether a special management group will be formed or whether there will be company wide participation?

13. Does the proposal show the position of the project manager or individual (company) in the overall company organization and the limits of authority and responsibility?

14. If no overall group is to be formed, does the proposal show the method of operation within the overall company structure?

15. Does the proposal delineate the requisite numbers (neither over-or-under managed) of the right types of proposal team members?

16. Where organizational charts are presented, is it clearly shown how the proposal team will operate effectively on a day to day basis?

17. If information furnished as to the type, frequency, and effectiveness of management controls and methods for corrective action?

18. Do manpower buildup charts clearly explain the methods of manpower acquisition, particularly skilled/specific manpower requirement?

19. Is a total manpower plan and individual plans engineering, manufacturing and QC furnished?

20. Is information furnished showing how the present project will phase in with current and future business?

21. If the proposal involves project management does the proposal show how the subcontractor's management will be integrated into the program?

22. Are organization charts furnished of first and second tier subcontractors which show clearly their relationship to the client to other subcontractors?

CHECKLIST—SUBCONTRACTORS PORTION OF PROPOSAL

1. This checklist must convince the client that we will apply the same controls to subcontractors as applies to the prime and must demonstrate the following:
    - ☐ A close coordination in planning stage
        - Firm definition of task
        - Monitoring of manpower
        - Rigidly controlled dollar allocation
        - Funding control related to milestones
        - Schedule and cost visibility through our method and type of planning format.
    - ☐ Communications
        - Face to face meetings
        - Procurement, QC, Engineering etc. assigned to contractor's plant.

2. This checklist must also show that if the complexity or size or importance of the contract requires it, we have the ability to perform the following additional procedures:
    - Evaluation of the acceptability of subcontract accounting, cost management reporting and configuration management techniques.
    - Wage and salary evaluation
    - Evaluation of overtime requirements
    - Evaluation of subcontract engineering change proposals
    - Evaluation of purchasing procedures

These guidelines will vary of course in application to individual projects, but they serve to identify potential trouble areas and thus minimize our exposure to future claims and/or labor problems.

CHECKLIST FOR SUBCONTRACT PREAWARD CONFERENCE

DOCUMENTS

1. Has bidder received all documents and drawings covering his work?
2. Question any exceptions to General Conditions
3. Review of Special Conditions
4. Review of specifications, page-by-page if warranted

EXPERIENCE—PERSONNEL—EQUIPMENT

1. Review of bidder's financial condition
2. Check on size of previous jobs
3. Check on type of previous jobs
4. References of recent customers
5. Who would be in responsible charge of work for bidder; can and will he focus on job?

6. Who would be his top field representative? What is this man's experience concerning:
   a. type of job
   b. methods of operation
   c. site conditions
   d. local labor relations

8. What organizational backup is available for top field representative?
9. Does bidder have necessary procurement and expediting procedures and capabilities?
10. Bidder should state all major construction equipment he intends to employ at site
11. Condition of this equipment
12. Timely availability of this equipment
13. What work does bidder plan to subcontract and to whom?

SCOPE

1. Has bidder included, all separate phases of intended scope; visual review of drawings?
2. Item-by-item check of quantities
3. Interfaces: does bidder understand the conditions at the start and finish of his scope of work; where his work stops and work of others begins?
   ☐ Examples
      i. cleaning of excavation
      ii. dewatering
      iii. weld-end preparation
      iv. method of shipment of items furnished, by others
      v. preoperational checkout
      vi. lubrication
      vii. necessary coordination with work of others
      viii. assurance of reasonable access

4. Review any changes in design, scope or intent since issue of inquiry not covered by addendum
5. Reiterate Owner's requirement for cleanup program

SCHEDULE OF WORK

1. Has the schedule of work changed since issue of inquiry?
2. Exceptions to START and COMPLETE dates; are these dates realistic?
3. Will bidder accept imposed overtime costs to complete per schedule?
4. Has bidder analyzed velocity of operation in regard to quantities of items to be installed in given time spans?
5. Has bidder considered manpower?

6. Precisely what are bidder's intentions as to how many of what crafts are required?
7. Does bidder have a bar chart or CPM schedule of his work; will he promptly produce one; do we have such a schedule for comparison?
8. Portions of work now, remobilize later (additional cost?)

LABOR RELATIONS

1. Project is Building Trades job
2. What crafts regularly employed by bidder?
3. Does bidder have experience with particular local unions having jurisdiction; which ones have signed agreements with you?
4. Recognized union for survey work
5. Are there items in scope of work requiring bidder to employ trades he does not regularly employ?
6. Detail check of bidder's intended assignments in jurisdictionally sensitive areas
7. Is stipulation for this project only?
8. In case bidder arbitrarily makes unreasonable misassignments of work, is he willing to accept full responsibility for any financial assessment imposed by Building Trades?
9. Will bidder accept and enforce the work rules as defined in the Work Rules Agreement between National Constructors Association and Building and Construction Trades Department?

COST ALLOCATION

1. Bidder should be told of our requirement that he break down his price into necessary parts for cost account purposes.
2. Manpower: has bidder included any premium monies to attract manpower and/or improve schedule.

COMMERCIAL

1. Escalation; what is precise basis for billing
2. Percentage of adders for bidder's work and bidder's sub-subcontrator work
3. Terms of payment
4. Sales and use taxes, separately stated
5. Insurance requirements/takeout
6. Unit prices for additions and deletions from lump-sum contracts
7. Investigation of areas of exposure to "extras"
8. Release of liens
9. Possible guaranteed maximum
10. Possible penalty/bonus; who participates; how
11. Supervisory personnel; actual salary; overtime treatment
12. Major equipment; repairs
13. Fee; what is included
14. Warranty of workmanship

CHAPTER 4

CONTRACT PACKAGES WITH
FLOW DIAGRAMS

Construction for Fast Track/Contract Package Mode can be utilized very easily on any size of construction project including the very large and complex projects such as Power House Projects.

In this chapter, a Power House Project has been used to develop a list of Contract Packages. A brief, but detailed description of each segment of work with a scope, specified work to be done by the contractor, work not included and QA/QC requirements. Following the description of each contract package, a flow diagram has been instituted from the time Architect/Engineers drawings and specs have been released for review until the time the contractor actually begins work.

1.0 TEMPORARY BUILDINGS-WAREHOUSES AND CHANGES HOUSES

15. Scope

The contractor shall provide all supervision, labor, new materials, tools, equipment and services to design, detail furnish, deliver, unload, protect, transport and erect pre-fabricated metal buildings and their accessories as shown on drawings and referenced in engineer's criteria specifications, including substructure foundation work associated with enumerated building structures and including all building services for each of the buildings. (Figure 5)

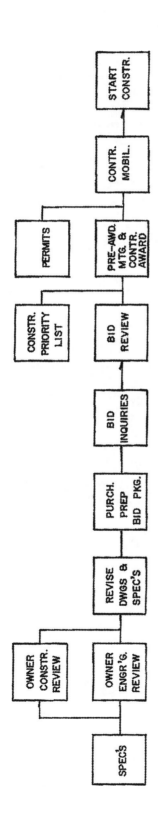

FIGURE #5

CONTRACT PACKAGE
TEMPORARY BUILDINGS

2.0 EXCAVATION

1.2 Scope

The contractor shall provide all supervision, labor, tools, miscellaneous materials and equipment to perform unclassified excavation, rock excavation, demolition and excavation slope protection for the following areas: (Figure 6)

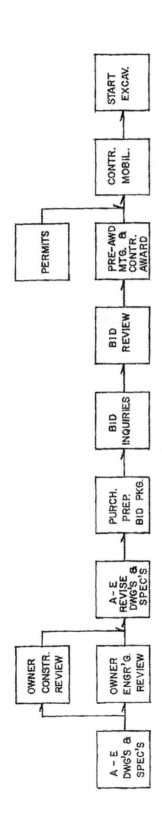

FIGURE #6

CONTRACT PACKAGE
EXCAVATION

    1.1 Boiler foundation and boiler house foundations
    1.2 Turbine pedestal foundation
    1.3 Turbine building foundation
    1.4 Circulating water pipe
    1.5 Control building foundation

1.2 Work by Contractor

    2.1 Unclassified excavation, rock excavation including blasting to limits and pay lines, as shown on drawing and in accordance with specifications.

    2.2 Protect and maintain slope of excavation as required.

    2.3 Contractor shall dispose of and/or store excavated material in areas shown on drawings and in accordance with direction of Construction Managers.

    2.4 Disposal of all trees, stumps, brush and other organic materials and debris in accordance with specifications and directions of the company representative.

    2.5 Blasting, if required, shall be preformed in a safe manner and all precautions required by Federal, State and Local codes shall be taken to protect the public, worker and property. Contractor shall excavate and control blast to pay lines and limits specified and shown on drawings. Any over blasting breakage beyond pay lines and limits shall be removed and replaced with fill concrete (class and strength to be specified) at contractor's expense. No reimbursement will be made for over excavation beyond specified depths and lines.

    2.6 Furnish all temporary facilities for his scope of work including portable power generators, compressors, etc.

    2.7 All surveying and layout from project, survey control points established by company representatives.

    2.8 Contractor shall clean up excavation of all deleterious materials including mud, broken or loose rock and leave surfaces workable to receive concrete mud mat.

    2.9 Contractor, if required, shall stabilized excavated surface to insure soil compaction as specified.

1.3 Work Not Included

    3.1 Installation of temporary power distribution system, temporary facilities electrical work, and maintenance of temporary electrical system.

    3.2 All form work, embedments, concrete work, etc., not specifically required of the excavation contractor shall be by others.

    3.3 Survey control points

    3.4 Site clearing and grubbing

    3.5 General grading

    3.6 Temporary road and parking areas

    3.7 Dewatering

3.0 CONCRETE 1

1.1 Scope

The contractor shall provide all supervision, labor, new materials, tools and equipment to construct the turbine building foundation, turbine building pedestal, boiler foundation and piers, boiler base slab, sand fill and cover slab, control building foundation, circulating water pipe support slab and miscellaneous foundation. (Figure 7)

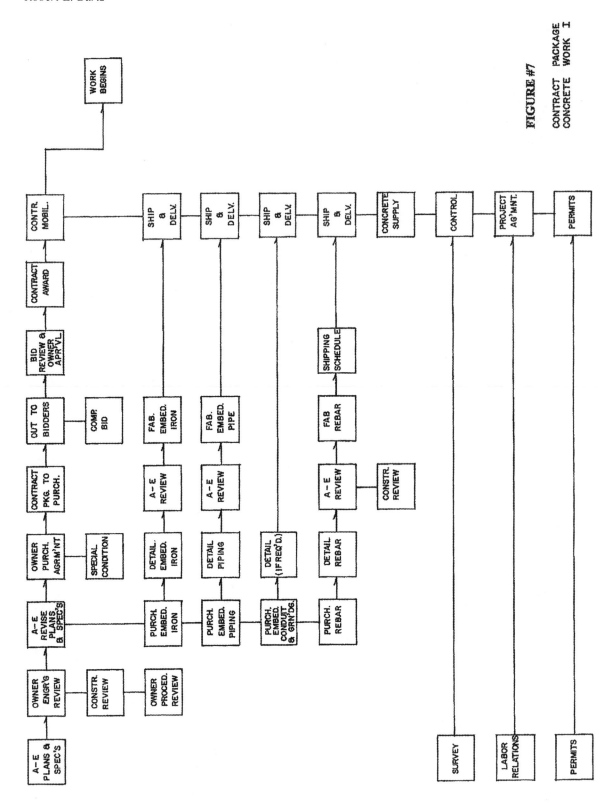

FIGURE #7

CONTRACT PACKAGE
CONCRETE WORK I

40

1.2 Work by Contractor

    2.1   Furnish and install formwork, and install all anchor bolts, miscellaneous steel and all embedded items, unload, protect, store and install reinforcing steel supplied by others, including dowels for subsequent work; install and place all concrete including finishes:

        2.1.1   Boiler building foundation, slab, perimeter walls, column foundations and column pedestals.

        2.1.2   Turbine-generator building base slab, perimeter walls, column foundations and column pedestals and pits and install support slab.

        2.1.3   Turbine-generator base and turbine-generator pedestal complete including installation of special anchor blocks furnished by T-G manufacturer, and including special anchor bolts and their templates.

        2.1.4   Control building foundation slab and column foundations.

        2.1.5   Install fill concrete and/ or mud mat as required to bring subgrades to proper elevation.

    2.1   Upload, store, handle and install embedded items including rough plumbing, piping, conduit, grounding, miscellaneous steel, anchor bolts, special anchor blocks for T-G foundations, inserts, etc.

    2.2   Furnish, operate and maintain dewatering equipment and provide necessary local pumping equipment as required to maintain dry subgrade conditions

    2.3   Maintain slopes and slope protection in accordance with drawings and as specified.

    2.4   Furnish and install all waterproofing for foundations and walls as specified.

    2.5   Backfill with selected materials, including compaction as specified, all foundations and structures in this scope of work. Rough grade to elevations shown on drawings.

    2.6   Provide complete and continuous inspection and reports for erection of forms, water stops, installation of resteel, embedments, special anchor blocks and anchor bolts, etc., as being in conformance with engineer's drawings, specifications and QA/QC procedures. All these inspection and inspection reports to be furnished by an approved test laboratory.

    2.7   All surveying and layout from project control points established by owner.

    2.8   All temporary facilities including field offices, change houses, warehouses and shops as required, power extension from load centers, compresses air, bottled gas and air, sanitary facilities including maintenance thereof until construction facilities are available, and drinking and construction water from designated onsite source.

1.3 Work Not Included

    3.1   Delivery and furnishing fabricated reinforcing steel

    3.2   Production and delivery of concrete

    3.3   Survey control points

    3.4   Furnishing special anchor blocks by T-G manufacturer

3.5 Intake structure, stack foundation, transformer foundations, discharge structure, service building, substation foundations, etc.

3.6 Furnish and install circulating water pipe

3.7 Furnish embedded materials including miscellaneous iron pipe, conduit, grounding, etc.

3.8 Furnish backfill material.

4.0 Construction Procedures and QA/QC Requirements

4.1 The contractor shall comply and conform to quality assurance requirements as delineated in the specification and referenced codes and standards.

4.2. Contractor shall submit for approval detailed written construction and inspection procedures as applicable to the contract scope of work.

4.3 The above data and detailed written construction procedures must be submitted to Construction Manager for approval before starting any phase of work within the scope of this contract.

4. TEMPORARY BUILDINGS-GUARDHOUSES, MAIN OFFICES AND TIME OFFICE

1.0 Scope

The contractor shall provide all supervision, labor new materials, tools, equipment and services to design, detail, furnish, deliver, unload, protect, transport and erect prefabricated metal building and accessories, as shown on drawings and referenced in engineer's criteria specifications, including substructure foundation work associated with enumerated building, and including all building required for the building. (Figure 8)

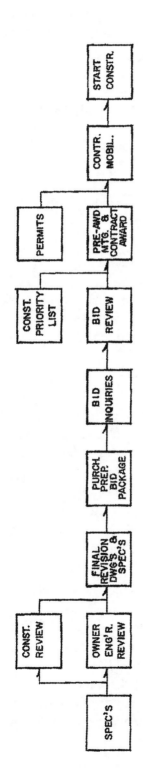

FIGURE #8

CONTRACT PACKAGE
TEMPORARY BUILDINGS

2.0 Work by Contactor

The work shall include but not be limited to the following:

  2.1 Prepare foundation areas including dewatering, maintenance and backfill.

  2.2 Design, detail, fabricate, deliver and erect all reinforcing steel, formwork and place concrete and finish all floor slabs, (concrete delivered by others), and furnish and place all embedded miscellaneous steel, anchor bolts, pipe, pipe sleeves, floor drains, sanitary service lines and sleeves, embedded conduit runs and grounding systems, inserts, outlets, junction boxes, anchors for each and all architectural items as specified.

  2.3 Erect prefabricated metal buildings including items as specified such as:

  2.3.1 Insulate exterior walls with metal faces insulated liner, or equal.

  2.3.2 Insulate roof with flexible fibre glass insulation over purlins with acoustical ceiling.

  2.3.3 Roof vents and ventilators with bird screens

  2.3.4 Paint interior walls and partitions.

  2.3.5 Install all glass, glazing and metal sash.

  2.3.6 Install all doors and door saddles, thresholds weather-stripping and submit hardware schedule for approval.

  2.3.7 Erect office partitions.

  2.3.8 All concrete floor slabs to be treated with non-dusting type finish.

  2.3.9 Install and erect stair stringers and treads.

  2.3.10 Furnish and install miscellaneous items such as millwork, cabinet work, wire screens, weather stripping and storm doors, all metal flashing and counter flashing for building

  2.3.11 Install window shades.

  2.3.12 Install steel shelving, bins and clockers.

  2.4 Building services required as specified by engineer's specifications such as:

  2.4.1 Install and test and place in service main electrical power distribution systems required for lighting and service outlets (110V and 220V).

  2.4.2 Heating and ventilation systems and louvers.

  2.4.3 Vents and ducts for blueprinting equipment roof.

  2.4.4 Install and test sanitary facilities complete for all buildings as specified including fixtures, mirrors, men and women toilet partitions in accordance with sanitary codes and local building code.

  2.4.5 Janitor's sink and closet.

  2.4.6 Install, test and place in service all portable water systems, including drinking fountains and drain and connect to designated source.

  2.4.7 Extend all sanitary lines three feet beyond building lines and test (connections to main sanitary systems by others).

  2.4.8 Install all gutter and roof drain as specified.

  2.4.9 Install, test and place in service a wet system for fire protection including an alarm system, complete fire fighting equipment, hoses, nozzles, hose cabinets, tie into and connect to permanent plant fire protection system installed by others or to the temporary construction fire protection system installed by others.

    2.4.10 Furnish and install temporary fuel tanks, pumps and piping.

2.5 Contractor shall be responsible for all surveys and layouts from project control points established by owner.

2.6 The contractor shall be responsible for compliance with all requirements of the Project Building Permit and execute the entire scope of work for this specification in accordance with engineer's criteria specification, all federal, state and local law and building codes and ordinances governing this project.

2.7 All designs of whatever nature for this contract shall be performed and executed by a licensed professional engineer registered in the state.

    2.7.1 All design dates, calculations, drawings, detailed sketches and other supporting design data must be submitted to the Construction Manager for approval.

    2.7.2 Approval by the owner's engineer does not relieve the contractor, his subcontractors and/or his architect-engineer from any responsibility for the adequacy of design and construction and safety of the structures under the laws of the state.

2.8 Furnish, erect and install all temporary facilities including offices, changehouses, warehouses and shops as required, power extensions from designated load centers, compressed air, bottled gas, all heating and temporary heat for protection of work for this contract, sanitary facilities and maintenance thereof, drinking and construction water from designated source.

5. TEMPORARY ELECTRICAL FACILITIES

1.0 Scope

The contractor shall provide all supervision, labor and tools (under $600.00 each value) to install the temporary electrical power transforming, switching and distribution and yard lighting, installation of temporary electrical power source of all construction building, fire systems, sewage treatment plant, temporary pumps, permanent equipment as required, etc., in accordance with drawings and specifications. Contractor shall maintain temporary electrical facilities until construction has been completed. (Figure 9)

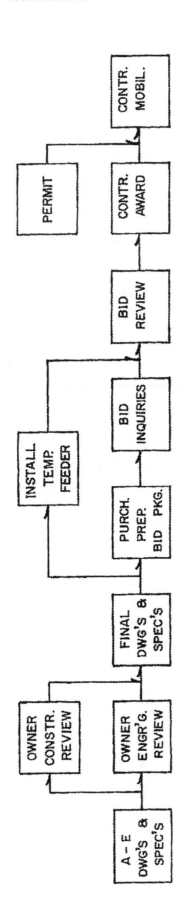

FIGURE #9

CONTRACT PACKAGE
TEMPORARY ELECTRICAL

46

3.9 Work by Contractor

    3.10 Install temporary electrical power transforming, switching and distribution equipment, temporary yard lighting and conduit, duct, cable and hardware as required. Temporary Load Centers, providing usable power for the general contractors, shall be installed where shown on the drawings.

    3.11 Electrical power source for all temporary facilities including offices, changehouses, warehouses and shops as specified and including maintenance thereof.

    3.12 The contractor will be required to map and locate new and now existing underground duct bank, conduit or buried power cables and any power systems he installs, or connects to Power company tie-line and/or equipment. A complete set of "as built" drawings must be furnished by this contractor to the Construction Manager.

    3.13 Maintain temporary electrical facilities during construction including but not limited to:

        3.13.1 Furnish and perform induction stress relieving

        3.13.2 Furnish and install temporary communication system

        3.13.3 Furnish and install temporary lighting

        3.13.4 Furnish and install temporary power for permanent equipment

        3.13.5 Furnish and install temporary welding distribution system in permanent buildings

        3.13.6 Perform minor repair of electrical equipment including welding machines.

    3.14 Contractor shall conform to all regulatory codes enumerated by all governing bodies.

    3.15 Surveying and layout from project survey control points established by the owner.

    3.16 All temporary facilities for temporary electrical facilities contractor including offices, changhouses, warehouses and shops as required, power from a temporary generating source as required; compressed air, bottled gas, sanitary facilities including maintenance thereof, and drinking and construction water from designated on site source.

    3.17 Contractor shall excavate, dewater and install miscellaneous foundations as required for temporary electrical.

1.4 Work Not Included

    4.1 Construction of permanent facilities

    4.2 Grounding except as required for temporary electrical work

    4.3 Survey control points

    4.4 Furnish new or used material and equipment

    4.5 Furnish and install fence enclosure

    4.6 Furnish concrete, reinforcing and embedments

    4.7 Furnish construction heavy equipment or small tools exceeding $600.00 each value

4.8 Furnish and maintain initial portable power generators used by contractors prior to energizing temporary distribution system.

6. BATCH PLANT FOR FURNISHING AND DELIVERY OF CONCRETE

1.0 Scope

The contractor shall provide all supervision, labor, materials, including cements, aggregates, air entrainments agents, and/or other admixtures as specified, tools and equipment including building and storage bins and the design of their foundations to produce and deliver all classes concrete required for the construction of the project. (Figure 10)

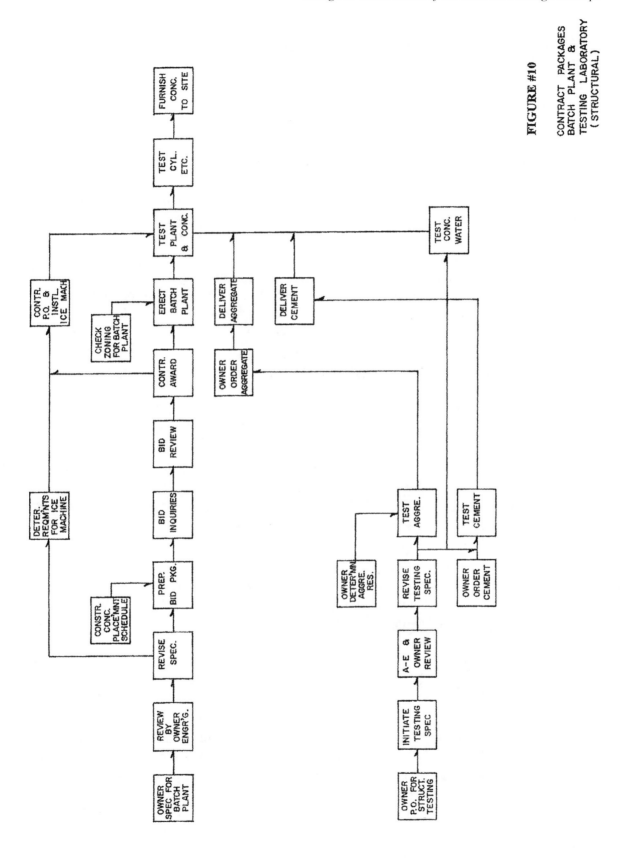

FIGURE #10

CONTRACT PACKAGES
BATCH PLANT &
TESTING LABORATORY
(STRUCTURAL)

2.0 General

It is the intent that the contractor shall operate his own central mix concrete producing facilities, and shall produce and deliver by truck-mixer the quantities required by the various contractors at the site upon due and proper notice. The contractor shall provide backup plant and equipment.

3.0 Work by Contractor

3.1 Provide all supervision, labor, new materials, tools and equipment to construct, operate and maintain the concrete producing facilities. This shall include at the central batch plant site maintenance of service roads foundations, extension of power and water from designated sources, if located on site and whatever else is required to construct a complete facility.

3.2 Provide all supervision, labor, materials, tools and equipment and perform whatever work is necessary to install, operate and maintain an aggregate producing plant at a site agreed to by the Owner.

3.3 Provide adequate equipment and facilities to properly stockpile, store, protect and prevent contamination from whatever source of all concrete materials. Individual piles to be stocked to maintain graduation segregation.

3.4 Both the central batch plant and aggregate producing plant must be adequately protected for continuous production of concrete. Provide the necessary equipment and/or materials to heat or cool stockpiles of aggregates and the concrete and supply within specified temperature ranges in accordance with referenced codes.

3.5 Provide sufficient labor and equipment to transport the concrete from the mixing plant to designated point of delivery.

3.6 Provide verification of design mixes for each class of concrete, and result of acceptance tests required by referenced codes or standards for all materials including cement, aggregates, water and admixtures.

3.7 The batch plant and the aggregate plant shall be located as shown on the drawings and /or as described in bidding documents.

3.8 Remove batch plant, aggregate plant foundations and any other Contractor provided site alterations and leave plant sites as specified and within the time specified upon completion of the contract (applicable if plant is located on site).

3.9 All surveying and layout for Batch Plant(s) from project survey control points established by Owner (applicable if plant is located on site).

3.10 All temporary facilities including offices, changehouses, warehouses, shops and heating plant equipment, parking area as required, power extension from load centers, compressed air, bottled gas and air sanitary facilities including maintenance thereof and snow removal there from and drinking and concrete producing facilities water from designated sources (if located on site).

4.0 Performance Requirements

   4.1   Plant Start-up
         The contractor shall submit for approval detailed test procedures to establish minimum and maximum mixing time and to determine performance of a stationary batch plant mixer. References used and test acceptance criteria shall be that detailed in ASTM Designation C94-69 and its latest addenda. The Construction Manager's test laboratory shall witness report on all conducted tests and submit a written report to the Construction Manager with a copy to the contractor.

   4.2   The concrete producing facility including the aggregate plant shall be complete and fully proof tested in time to produce the required verification of design mixes at the minimum rate of production specified elsewhere in this specification. (Design mixes to be supplied by engineer.) Approval of the production facilities shall include demonstration of plants' capability to produce concrete classes of strengths, slumps and workability characteristics of concrete as specified by the established design mixes.

   4.3   Concrete Plant Capacity
         The concrete plant shall be capable of producing a minimum _____ cubic yards per hour based on a 90 second mixing time, with a capability of producing _____ cubic yards during an eight hour period. Trucks shall be available to deliver concrete at _____ cubic yards per hour, or_____ cubic yards per hour when the backup plant is also in service (see Paragraph 7.0).

   4.4   Aggregate Supplier
         The aggregate plant shall be of sufficient size and capacity to permit full capacity and range of operation of the concrete plant(s), and meet ASTM requirements for aggregate producing facilities.

5.0 Delivery

   The contractor shall deliver concrete to the construction contractors into chutes, buckets or whatever. Access across the construction site to the point of truck discharge shall be provided by the construction contractors; however, this contractor is to assure himself that access is satisfactory.

   5.1   The contractor shall not be required to furnish concrete orders for less than one cubic yard. For larger orders, concrete shall be furnished in increments of one half yard.

   5.2   The contractor shall establish a time and a priority by which concrete orders must be placed for delivery for the following day. Any conflicts shall be referred to the Construction Manager for resolution, with priorities to be established on a day to day basis as required.

   5.3   Delivery tickets shall accompany each load of concrete and shall contain the following information:
         a.   Name of owner
         b.   Name of contractor or individual who placed order, date, time, weather, temperature and quantity

  c. Ticket serial number
  d. Truck number
  e. Load number
  f. Date and time load batched
  g. Class and quantity of concrete
  h. Batch mix identification
  i. Location of pour
  j. Ice-pounds and gallons
  k. Truck revolution counter-reading at time of truck charging

5.4 Copies of the delivery ticket to be furnished to the consignee, the owner's QA representative and the Construction Manager.

5.5 All information produced on the mixer ticket or tape shall be attached to the QA representative's copy of the delivery ticket.

5.6 Concrete trucks shall be of the rapid discharge "high dump" type, meet ASTM requirements for truck mixers and be rated at a minimum of 8 cubic yards mixing capacity of larger to meet the primary concrete plant single or even multiple batch capacity.

5.7 Contractor shall dispose of excess concrete in areas agreed to by the owner.

6.0 Batching

6.1 The central mix-plant(s) shall be semi automatic or better.

6.2 Separate bins or compartments shall be provided for the aggregate, for different sizes of coarse aggregate and for bulk cement when used. The compartments shall be sized and constructed to preclude intermingling of the various materials. Separate silos shall be required for each type of cement, as specified.

6.3 A suitable water measuring device shall be used which will also contain an interlock to prevent discharging before the filling valve is fully closed. The method of delivering water to the mixer shall be so designated that leakage will not occur. When admixtures are used, a proper separate measuring and dispersing device for each admixture shall be used.

6.4 In order to readily control water requirements in the mix caused by changes in the moisture in the aggregate, a moisture compensator shall be installed.

6.5 Accurate measurement of the concrete ingredients is essential. The scales shall be calibrated upon completion of the erection of the plant and checked by an independent agency every four to six weeks thereafter as specified, and in accordance with applicable standards. A printout shall contain the weights of all ingredients used in the mix as well as the mix designation, time and date.

6.6 When ice is used in the concrete mix, suitable equipment shall be used to shred, weigh and record the quantity used.

6.7 All weighing, indicating recording and control equipment shall be adequately protected against exposure to dust and weather.

7.0 Backup Equipment

A backup plant shall be provided which is capable of producing cubic yards per hour, based on a 90 second mixing time with a capability of producing cubic yards during an eight hour period, with detail requirements the same as primary batch plant-Section 6.0.

8.0 Quality Assurance Requirements

    8.1 The contractor shall submit his complete quality assurance procedures as required by specifications.

    8.2 The contractor shall submit quality assurance procedures as required by the specifications.

    8.3 The contractor shall submit for approval and /or record documentation as follows:

        a. Concrete design mix verification reports

        b. Concrete test reports including slump, air content, temperature and unit weight.

        c. Material test reports and/or certifications.

        d. Central mixing plant operations records.

        e. Material analysis and physical property reports for fine and coarse aggregate and admixtures as required

        f. Water chemical analysis reports.

        g. Calibration of test equipment and mixing plant calibration procedures and reports.

        h. Corrective action reports

    8.4 Basis for rejection of concrete materials or concrete shall be as specified.

9.0 Sampling and Testing

Sampling and testing all materials at the central mix plant and aggregate plant to maintain conformance with the specifications shall be the responsibility of the owner.

    9.1 Sampling and testing fine and coarse aggregates shall be performed as specified by the contractor and monitored by the Owner/Construction Manager.

    9.2 Cement shall be tested by the supplier with copies of the mill test certificates for each shipment transmitted to the Owner/Construction Manager.

    9.3 Cement supplied in bulk from a single mill shall be of uniform color. Mixing of different suppliers' cements in silos should be avoided.

10.0 Work Not Included

    10.1 Placement of concrete, including equipment, between truck delivery point and the forms.

    10.2 Establishment of design mixes.

    10.3 Electric power and water (if located on site).

10.4 Project control survey points (if located on site).

10.5 Clearing, general grading, roadwork and parking area, except as noted (if located on site).

10.6 Testing laboratory.

FIELD TESTING LABORATORY SERVICES (STRUCTURAL)

1.1 Scope

This contractor and his supervisory personnel shall be conversant with and knowledgeable of Quality Assurance criteria for Fossil Fuel Power Plants and other standards and governing codes as applicable to this scope of work, as well as demonstrated experience in performing laboratory test services required for the field of nuclear generating power plant's construction. The Contractor shall furnish all supervision, labor, tools, new materials and calibrated instruments and test equipment to perform all onsite laboratory testing services associated with quality control of concrete materials, high strength bolting and user testing for reinforcing steel, soils and rock testing. Prepare and distribute test reports and data as specified.

1.2 Work By Contractor

2.1 Furnish and install test equipment necessary to operate a laboratory for testing of aggregates and concrete.

2.2 Obtain and transport samples to the test laboratory.

2.3 Store, cure and test samples.

2.4 Provide continuous inspection services at the batch plant(s) and aggregate producing plant(s).

2.5 Witness the testing of fine and coarse aggregates as specified, including inspection of sources of aggregate.

2.6 Provide field inspection of concrete delivered to the jobsite, for compliance with Engineer's specifications and QA/QC criteria as specified.

2.7 Provide surveillance inspection for high strength bolting during the structural steel erection period.

2.8 Provide for periodic "users" testing of reinforcing steel in the field or in home office laboratory as required.

2.9 Provide field tests for soils classification, soil compaction and moisture content as specified.

2.10 Provide test data and reports on site rock samples as specified.

2.11 Prepare and distribute reports as required by the specifications.

2.12 Furnish and maintain and operate a pickup truck for use at the site for transporting aggregate and concrete samples to the test laboratory.

1.3 Work Not Included

1.1 Source of water and electric service for test facility furnished by others (if lab is on site).

1.4 Specifications and QA/QC Criteria Specifications
Referenced codes, standards and specifications shall be the latest revision at the time of bidding.

1.5 Contractor Furnished Equipment
  5.1 The Contractor shall equip the testing laboratory with adequate facilities for testing aggregates and curing and testing concrete samples and cylinders associated with a batch plant capacity of cubic yards per eight hour day.
  5.2 The Contractor shall maintain the testing laboratory and its equipment in first class working order. The premises shall be neat and orderly at all times.

6.0 Sampling and Testing
The Contractor shall be responsible for obtaining samples and performing tests in accordance with referenced codes, standards and specifications, as specified.

7.0 Laboratory Schedule
  7.1 The Contractor shall have the test facility equipment installed and ready for use immediately after receiving notice to proceed from the Owner. It is anticipated that the quality control test facility will be required as directed.
  7.2 The testing program will require the services of an Engineer and Chief Technician from 30 to 46 months and assistants for a period of approximately 48 months. Their assistants will be employed on an as required basis and subject to the approval of the Owner's representative. Contractor's employees shall be experienced in this class of work and part of his regular staff. The Contractor shall submit resumes of all employees associated with this contract.

8.0 Inspection
The Owner and/or Construction Manager shall have free access to the testing facilities during working hours and to inspect and observe the tests being performed.

9.0 Supervision
All services shall be under the supervision of a Professional Engineer registered in the state.

7. Pipe installation

1.0 Scope
The Contractor shall furnish all supervision, labor services, new materials, tools (under $600.00 value) instruments, supplies, equipment to install prefabricated onsite piping and/or fabricated onsite piping as required, expedite, receive, unload, store, protect, remove from storage, transport, rig, install, checkout, test and make ready for operation the piping systems, valves, and piping specialties including engineered pipe hanger systems, field fabricated pipe hanger systems and supplemental supporting structural steel for hangers.

Scope of work shall include but not be limited to the following systems: Main Steam, Main Feedwater, Auxiliary Feedwater, Auxiliary Boiler, Diesel Generator, Diesel

Fuel Oil Storage and Transfer, BOP Service Water, Nitrogen Gas, Demineralizer Water Makeup, Condensate Storage, Moisture Separator Reheater Drain, H2 and CO2 Supply, Feedwater Drain, Chilled Water, Primary Gas, Primary Water, Vents and Drains, Component Cooling, Hydrogen Control, Chemical Addition, Portable Water.

The installation of complete sanitary systems in buildings designated including all piping, fixtures and accessories. The installation of all building roof drains and drain piping within building specified. All work shown on drawings and specified for complete pluming systems for the project except embedded items. (Figures 11, 12 & 13)

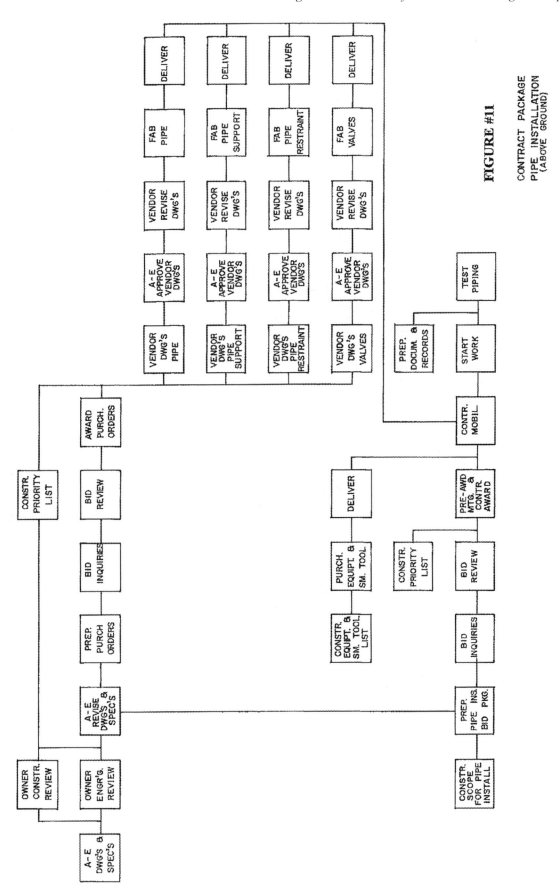

FIGURE #11

CONTRACT PACKAGE
PIPE INSTALLATION
(ABOVE GROUND)

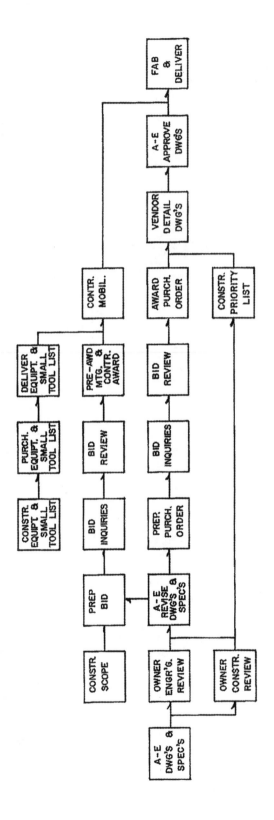

FIGURE #12

CONTRACT PACKAGE
UNDERGROUND PIPING

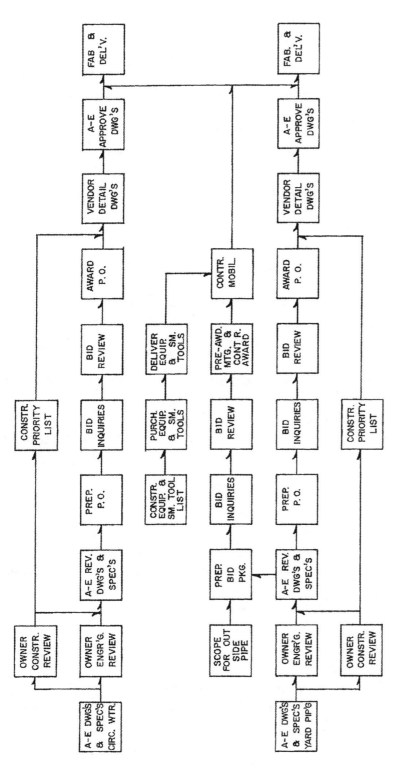

FIGURE #13

CONTRACT PACKAGE
UNDERGROUND PIPING

2.0 Work By Contractor

2.1 The Contractor shall be responsible for receiving and verifying and recording all material documentation as required by all applicable codes, standards, and Quality Assurance/Quality Control standards described elsewhere in Engineer's Specification.

2.2 The Contractor shall perform and/or provide test laboratory services to complete all nondestructive tests required and document the results of all tests in accordance with applicable codes, specifications, standards and QA/AC procedures.

2.3 The Contractor shall erect all piping as enumerated by systems, including all valves, piping specialties, engineered hanger systems and field fabricated hanger systems.

2.4 The erection of piping systems shall include but not be limited to hanging, protecting, alignment, fit-up with alignment templates and/or devices if required, welding, stress relieving, and cleanup. Provide labor to hydrostatically test and flush completed systems and disposal of water from tested systems. Provide labor for acid cleaning and flushing of certain piping systems.

2.5 Some isometric piping sketches will be forwarded to Contractor; remaining isometrics for all piping systems shall be prepared by the Contractor and forwarded to Engineer as specified.

2.6 Contractor shall erect all pipe hangers and supplemental support steel for hangers, seismic and/or jet force restraints, supports, valves, appurtenances and pipe specialties furnished and fabricated by others as enumerated by system.

2.7 Contractor shall fabricate and erect all small diameter piping, including preparations of isometrics drawings.

2.8 The Contractor shall submit to Engineer for approval all welding procedures and certified test laboratory data sheets for each and every welding procedure used. Contractor must quality all procedures as required by Engineer's specification, and ASME Code Section III and IX and other applicable sections of ASME Codes, or standards referenced.

2.9 Contractor shall provide and maintain a map and weld records of each and every weld for each piping system, showing location of weld, weld identifying number, welder(s) number and name, preheat data stress relieving, post heat data and charts, inspection data sheet for each weld and/or passes to complete weld, repairs and repair procedures used, physical and chemical analyses of weld metal.

2.10 Contractor shall set all permanent equipment with pipe fitter jurisdiction.

2.11 Contractor shall provide for Engineer's review and approval procedures shall include and preparation and fit-up and alignment methods and/or devices used to meet code tolerances as specified.

2.12 The Contractor shall complete each system fully, clean, test adjust and set hangers in cold and/or hot position prior to turn over for preoperational testing.

2.13 Contractor shall assist in start up operation as specified.

2.14 Contractor shall install all temporary piping distribution systems.

2.15 Work included for finished plumbing-The major sections of buildings in which work is included are: Service Building, Administration Building, Control Building, Turbine Room, and Heater Bay. The work shall include but not be limited to the following:

    2.15.1 Receiving, delivering, unloading, installing, insulating as required and initially operating and testing of all equipment and systems specified by the Engineer.

    2.15.2 Preparation of fabrication and erection drawings for piping systems specified including supports and hanger systems for equipment and piping supplied.

    2.15.3 Plumbing-sanitary systems required for this scope shall include but not be limited to the following:

        2.15.3.1 All Plumbing Fixtures and equipment.

        2.15.3.2 Electric water heaters, sanitary soil, waste (Underground sanitary piping) and vent piping, domestic hot and cold water piping and pipe insulation as per schedules.

        2.15.3.3 Roof drains and roof drainage piping, underground and floor slab drains, drainage piping, sumps and sump pumps, except embedded items.

        2.15.3.4 Instrument air, laboratory, air vacuum demineralized water, oxygen, hydrogen, helium, nitrogen, gas and/or other gas piping systems to laboratory fixtures and equipment shown on drawings or as specified.

        2.15.3.5 Install all laboratory fixtures and equipment supplied by others.

        2.15.3.6 All tanks and unfired pressure vessels (ASME stamped if required).

2.16 Contractor shall install and test all exposed rough and finished plumbing, including fixtures.

2.17 Complete all backfilling of trenches after successfully testing piping systems.

2.18 Install all piping insulation as specified for systems.

2.19 All surveying and layout from project survey control points established by Owner.

2.20 Power extension from load centers, compressed air, bottled gas and air, sanitary facilities including maintenance thereof until construction facilities are in service, and drinking and construction water from designated onsite source and connections to and from source of demineralized water for test purposes and disposal of demineralized water upon completion of specified tests.

3.0 Code Compliance and Standards.

All construction, design, fabrication and tests shall comply with all applicable state and local codes, laws, regulations or ordinances and with rules of the Board of Fire Underwriters.

1.6 Testing and Adjusting

6.1 The Contractor shall test hydrostatically all soil, waste, vent rain water and domestic hot and cold water piping systems in accordance with standard procedures and state and local regulations and codes.

6.2 Contractor shall test all air, vacuum, oxygen, hydrogen, nitrogen and other gas piping systems as specified.

6.3 All piping systems shall be tested and made tight before covering, enclosing in other construction or insulating.

6.4 Contractor shall make all necessary adjustments to equipment to ensure proper operation as specified.

6.5 All safety devices shall be checked, tested and set for proper and safe relieving pressures.

1.7 Construction Procedures and QA/QC Requirements

7.1 The Contractor shall comply and conform to quality Assurance requirements as delineated in the specifications referenced codes and standards.

7.2 The Contractor shall submit for approval his complete Quality Assurance Program which shall be in conformance with Quality Assurance Criteria Fossil Fuel for Power Plants.

7.3 Contractor shall submit detailed Quality Assurance Control procedures as required by the Engineer's specification.

7.4 Contractor shall initiate construction installation procedures in detail for the work within his scope. The procedures shall include but not be limited to the following; erection of materials in conformance with specifications, drawings, codes, welding procedures including operator and process welding procedures, certified data sheets of welding procedures, stress relieving procedures, erection sequence and shop fabrication procedures and controls, quality control check-list, calibration of test equipment and tools, alignment and erection tolerances and calibration of test equipment and tools, alignment and erection tolerances and calibration field precision instruments.

7.5 Construction procedures shall conform to applicable codes and Engineer's specifications. All construction installation procedures shall be reviewed by the Construction Managers; work shall not start until procedures have been reviewed and approved in writing. A deviation from approved procedures will require an addendum which must be approved in writing by the Construction Managers prior to resuming the specified work in question.

7.6 The Contractor shall perform all work in accordance with specifications, drawings, including notes thereon, referenced specifications, all applicable codes and procedures, and in conformance with all local, state and federal codes and regulations. Submittals of materials and drawings shall be as specified elsewhere in the contract documents.

1.8 Work Not Included

    8.1   Furnishing of all pipe, fittings, valves, pipe specialties and appurtenances, pipe hangers, support steel for supplemental supports of pipe hangers and / or equipment and plumbing fixtures and any incidentals thereto, including toilet partitions, screens, miscellaneous fixtures, drinking fountains, coolers and all other associated equipment.

    8.2   Electrical work and electrical power wiring of equipment.

    8.3   Cutting and patching of certain openings in walls or ceilings of various buildings and concrete structures.

    8.4   Equipment not included:

        8.4.1   Sewage disposal equipment supplied and listed by Owner.

        8.4.2   Laboratory equipment-water treatment.

        8.4.3   Kitchen equipment

        8.4.4   Instrument repair shop-equipment, sinks, water coolers, traps, tanks, etc.

    8.5   Survey control points.

    8.6   Temporary power distribution system, temporary facilities electrical work, and maintenance of temporary electrical facilities.

    8.7   Construction of sewage disposal plant and settling basin structures.

    8.8   Furnish and install instrumentation.

    8.9   Piping and appurtenances embedded in concrete.

    8.10 Furnish and install yard piping including circulating water pipe.

    8.11 Installation of piping except plumbing.

    8.12 Painting of piping and appurtenances.

    8.13 Work associated with condenser.

    8.14 Furnish welding electrodes.

OUTSIDE PIPING

1.1 Scope

The Contractor shall provide supervision, labor and tools (under $600.00 each value) to unload, store and protect, transport, erect, test and place in service all temporary and permanent outside piping for fire protection, portable water, waste water, including all circulating water piping within the buildings to condenser expansion joints and service water supply and return line connections, fuel oil, steam and condense piping including insulation for these systems, air demineralized water. The erection and installation of fire pumps including instrumentation and control piping systems, and associated equipment and tanks including complete foundations, structures, electrical and building services required to place in service the fir protection system.

2.0 Work By Contractor

The work shall include but not be limited to the piping systems, equipment and materials as follows:

2.1 The Contractor shall furnish the Construction Manager, prior to start of work and field fabrication and installation of pipe, information as follows: copies, if required, of all ASME Certificates of authorization for us of "P-P", "N", "NPT" and other ASME stamps for field fabrication and erection of piping and/or installation of components, and other piping systems whether installed by this Contractor. In addition, quality control procedures and erection procedures for all classes of work as defined in the "Scope of Work" must be submitted to the Construction Manager prior to start of work. Copies of Welding Procedures Qualification Data Sheets and Welding Process, and copies of each welder's Qualification Data Sheet and Process to which he has been qualified as required by applicable sections of the ASME Code and/or other referenced codes, must be submitted to the Construction Manager before proceeding with the field installation of piping systems. The contractor shall be responsible for receipt of material documentation, performing and/or providing for nondestructive testing and documentation thereof in accordance with applicable codes, specifications and quality assurance and quality control procedures. Procedures for maintenance and protection of materials in storage is a requirement

1.2 The Contractor shall erect all piping as enumerated by systems, including hangers, anchors, anchor blocks and/or restraints where required. The erection shall include handling, protecting, alignment, welding, stress relieving, and provide labor and portable water for hydrostatically testing piping systems and disposal of test water. Some isometrics may be forwarded to Contractor; remaining spool sheets and/or isometrics for all piping systems to be prepared by Contractor and forwarded to him as specified.

1.3 The Contractor shall erect all pipe hangers, seismic and/or jet force restraints, anchor blocks and supports, valves, appurtenances and piping specialties fabricated by others as enumerated by system.

1.4 The Contractor shall completely install the outside portion of the fire protection system for the project which will include the following: Contractor shall install fire protection system including two (2) 30,000 gallon aboveground storage tanks, pumps, hangers, pipe, instrumentation, valves, hoses, etc.

1.5 Install well water, service water and fire protection system in the yard area including fire hydrants, hose and hose housed, PIV's and valve boxes, and backfill as specified.

1.6 Contractor shall maintain records for each field weld identifying the welding operation, preheat, postheat, inspection, repair, weld metal, physical and chemical documentation, etc.; Contractor shall also provide welding procedures and be responsible for qualifications and/or codes. The Contractor shall furnish the Construction Manager at completion of work an "as built" set of marked up prints and/or sketches showing all field weld locations, numbers and identification marks, radiographs, if required, and complete history of each and every weld repair, for all piping systems which have welded joint construction. Included with this weld history, all results of hydrostatic or other NDT results must be documented and included.

1.7 Contractor shall clean, adjust and test all piping systems prior to turnover for preoperational testing.

1.8 Install potable water piping and waste water piping in the yard area, together with other yard piping and backfill as specified.

1.9 Flushing, cleaning and chlorination of potable water piping system shall be in accordance with specifications and local codes having jurisdiction.

1.10 Contractor shall install all interconnecting piping between circulating water piping and service water piping systems in yard area and terminate within building to limits as shown on drawings or as specified.

1.11 The excavation and backfilling of all pipe trenches and/or foundations shall be in accordance with the specifications and/or applicable referenced codes.

1.3 Work Not Included

3.1 Furnishing of fire pumps, and their associated equipment and instrumentation and control systems.

3.2 Long electrical conduit and wiring. Wiring in trays and long runs to control room for alarms and indication and power supplied by others.

3.3 All remote alarms.

3.4 Manufacturer's Service Engineers.

3.5 Special shop fabricated storage tanks.

3.6 Circulating water tunnels

3.7 Supply of piping materials, except as specified.

3.8 Pipe and plumbing within temporary buildings.

3.9 Furnish welding electrodes.

3.10 Furnish and maintain heavy construction equipment.

3.11 Furnish concrete, reinforcing and embedments.

1.7 GENERAL CONCRETE II

1.8 Scope

The Contractor shall furnish all supervision, labor services, tools (under $600.00 each value) to construct the intake structure, discharge structure, service building concrete, turbine and boiler superstructure concrete, transformer and switchyard foundations, miscellaneous building foundations, stack foundation, equipment foundations, concrete for duct bank etc. (Figure 14)

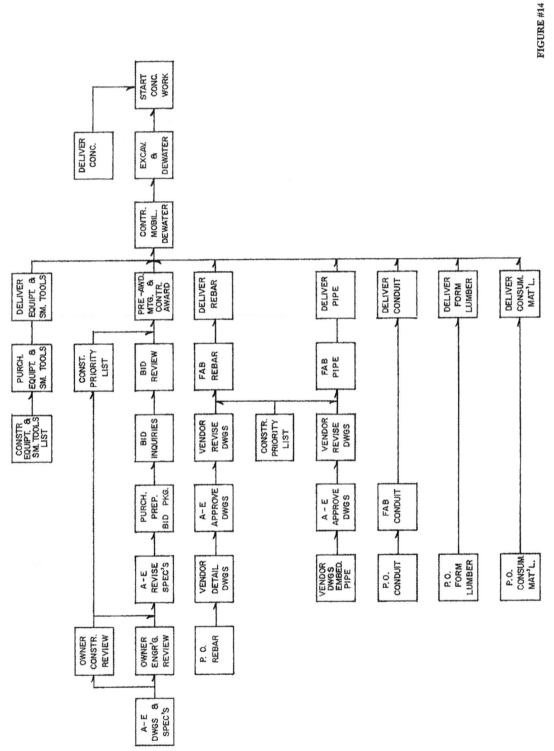

FIGURE #14

CONTRACT   PACKAGE
CONCRETE   II

Work By Contractor

    8.1   Furnish and install all formwork and install embedded materials, conduits, grounding, rough plumbing, pipe sleeves, pipe anchor bolts, miscellaneous steel, special inserts, reinforcing steel and placing concrete furnished by others.

    8.2   Furnish and install waterproofing for walls and tunnel passages below grade as specified.

    8.3   Furnish and install rails in heater bay floor slabs where called for and specified.

    8.4   Grouting of all structural steel base plates for structures specified.

    8.5   Surveying and layout of work from survey control points established by Owner

    8.6   Power extension from load centers, compressed air, bottled gas and air, sanitary facilities and maintenance thereof until such time as sanitary facilities are in service and drinking and construction water from designated on site source.

    8.7   Provide continuous and complete inspection and reports for forms, reinforcing steel, cad weld splice installations, and concrete placement for first level QA/QC requirements, inspections and reports as specified.

    8.8   All equipment construction openings and closure of same when directed.

    8.9   Furnish and install metal floor decking.

    8.10 Excavate, dewater and backfill as required.

    8.11 Backfill to grade.

1.9 Work Not Included

    9.1   Turbine foundation, pedestal and piers, boiler foundation and piers, boiler cover slab, miscellaneous foundations boiler area.

    9.2   Piping, electrical and plumbing work, except embedments specified.

    9.3   Turbine Building and Primary Auxiliary Building walls, roof and metal decking, structural steel(other than floor support system), floor grating, miscellaneous steel, except embedments specified, roofing and/or any of the finishes and architect trades items of work.

    9.4   Erection of any mechanical equipment.

    9.5   Production and delivery of concrete.

    9.6   Fabrication and delivery of reinforcing steel.

    9.7   Furnish special inserts for Owner furnished equipment.

    9.8   Materials testing.

    9.9   Electric power, water and sanitary facilities.

    9.10 Temporary construction office, changehouse and warehouse.

    9.11 Furnish and maintain heavy construction equipment.

    9.12 Furnish embedded metal, pipe, conduit, etc.

1.10 Construction Procedures and QA/QC Requirements

    10.1 The Contractor shall comply and conform to Quality Assurance requirements as delineated in the specification and referenced codes and standards.

10.2 The Contractor shall submit for approval his complete Quality Assurance Program which shall be in performance with Quality Assurance Criteria for Fossil Fuel Power Plants.

10.3 Contractor shall submit detail Quality Assurance and control procedures as required by Engineer's specification.

10.4 Contractor shall submit for approval detailed written construction and inspection procedures as applicable to the contract scope of work.

10.5 The above date and detailed written construction procedure must be submitted to the Engineer for approval before starting any phase of work within the scope of this contract.

9. BOILER ERECTION

1.0 Scope

The Contractor shall design, fabricate and provide supervision, labor and selective equipment to erect, test and place in service the Natural Circulation Steam Generator, including supporting structural steel, platforms, stairs, etc., fans, flues, duct, burners, soot blowers, mechanical dust collector, thermocouples and controls. (Figure 15)

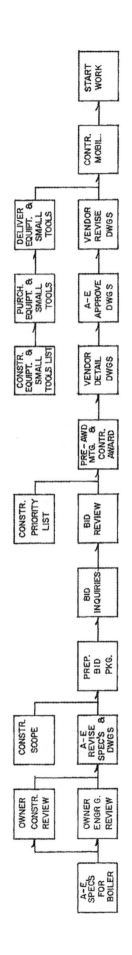

FIGURE #15

CONTRACT PACKAGE
BOILER ERECTION

2.0 Work By Contractor

    2.1   Design, fabricate and erect complete steel for the steam generators including base plates, high strength bolts, platforms, walkways, stairs, handrail and shop coat of paint.

    2.2   Furnish and install Superheat and Reheat Control systems including recorders and controllers, control valves, control drives for dampers and remote selector stations.

    2.3   Furnish and install Regenerative Air Heaters including all driving mechanism with speed reducer and electric motor, inspection ports and lights, heating elements and steam coils.

    2.4   Furnish and install the following flues and ducts:

        2.4.1   Economizer to air heaters.

        2.4.2   Air heaters to dust collector.

        2.4.3   Dust collector to I.D. fans.

        2.4.4   Flue gas inspection system.

        2.4.5   Soot hoppers.

        2.4.6   F.D. fans to air heaters.

        2.4.7   Air heaters to windbos.

        2.4.8   Overfire air ports and dampers.

        2.4.9   Furnish and install isolation dampers for air heaters including air flow measuring devices and expanded metal screen.

    2.5   Furnish and install insulation as specified.

    2.6   Furnish and install burner equipment and windboxes including oil burners, mechanical atomizing oil guns, BTG board inserts, local burner control stations, logic cabinets, prefabricated cable and wire solenoid valves, light oil transfer valve assemblies, oil valve assembly completely wired to a common junction box.

    2.7   Furnish and install fan equipment including control and starter equipment, electrical wiring, steam piping and valves for fan drive.

    2.8   Furnish and install motor operated soot blowing equipment including 5,000 gallon tank, surrey pump and agitator, controls, reducing station, motorized stop valve, main and branch pipe lines.

    2.9   Furnish and install Mechanical Dust Collector including separating elements, insulation, and water washing equipment.

    2.10 furnish and install thermocouples and electric motor driven thermo probes.

    2.11 Furnish and install piping (superheater outlet, reheater inlet and outlet and economizer inlet) to a point 3' outside of the boiler casing.

    2.12 Furnish only superheater and reheater safety valves and feed stop and check valves.

    2.13 Furnish and install drain and sample connections (terminate at main operating floor).

    2.14 Contractor shall perform hydrostatic and tightness tests.

    2.15 Contractor shall assist startup and train operating personnel.

2.16 Selective equipment furnished by contractor includes stiff leg derricks, x-ray trailers, 3 drum hoisting engines, 2 drum air hoist and elevator.

2.17 The Contractor shall submit to Engineering for approval all welding procedures and certified test laboratory data sheets for each and every welding procedure used. Contractor must qualify all welders to the specified approved procedures as required by engineer's specification, and ASME Code Section III and IX and other applicable sections of ASME Codes, or standards referenced.

2.18 Contractor shall provide and maintain a map and weld record of each and every weld, showing location of weld, weld identification number, welder(s) number and name, preheat data stress relieving, post heat data and charts, inspection data sheet for each weld and/or passes to complete weld, repairs and repair procedures used, physical and chemical analysis of weld metal.

2.19 Contractor shall furnish an authorized boiler inspection and insurance agency.

3.0 Work Not Included

   3.1   Foundations.

   3.2   Furnish construction tools and equipment (except as specified).

   3.3   Install railroad track, road and fence.

   3.4   Unload, hauling and handling between the points of free delivery of common carrier and the site of erection.

   3.5   Furnish welding electrodes.

   3.6   Furnish fuel, water, gases and oxygen, compressed air, and electrical power.

   3.7   Structural steel other than Boiler Structure.

   3.8   Installation Permits.

   3.9   Superheat and reheat control interconnecting wiring, connecting pipe and tubing, air compressors, filters, etc., as required for installation.

   3.10 Regenerative air heater electrical connections and starter for driving motor, piping and valves for water lines to and from bearing water connections. Cleaning and washing devices.

   3.11 Duct from I.D. fans to stack.

   3.12 All burner front piping and trip valves.

   3.13 I.D. & F.D. fan drives and damper drives.

   3.14 Slurry piping for soot blowers and electrical wiring external to equipment.

   3.15 Mechanical dust collector discharge valves.

   3.16 Thermocouples in excess of 150, recording instruments and wiring.

   3.17 Install feed stop and check valves.

   3.18 Furnish and erect water wash piping for furnace.

   3.19 Furnish and install burner piping.

   3.20 Furnish and install piping, drains and traps from steam coils.

   3.21 Survey control points.

   3.22 Finish painting.

10. MISCELLANEOUS STEEL

1.0 Scope

The Contractor shall provide all supervision, labor, tools (under $600.00 each value) materials to detail, fabricate, deliver, unload, store and/or transport and install steel stairs and/or ladders, miscellaneous platforms, grating and/or checker plate and handrail as shown on the drawings. Apply prime shop coat as required. (Figure 16)

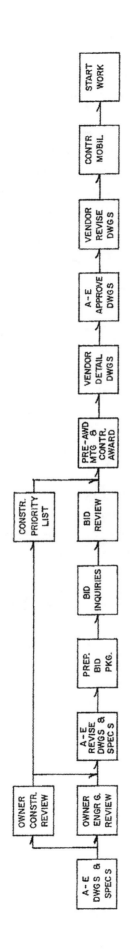

FIGURE #16

CONTRACT PACKAGE
MISCELLANEOUS STEEL

2.0 Work By Contractor

The work shall include but not be limited to the following:

2.1 Fabricate, furnish and install the steel stairs, platforms, grating and/or checker place in the Diesel Generator Building, Control Room, Administration and Service Building, Turbine Building, Circulating Water Pump House, etc.

2.2 Surveying and layout from project control points established by the Owner.

2.3 All temporary facilities including field offices, changehouses, warehouses and shops as required, supply compressed air, bottled gas, power extension from load centers until construction facilities are available, and water from designated onsite source.

3.0 Work Not Included.

3.1 Building structural steel framing.

3.2 Steel stairs, with handrails, which are supported from the structural steel.

3.3 Embedded miscellaneous steel.

3.4 Materials testing.

3.5 Electric power, water and sanitary facilities.

3.6 Project survey control points.

3.7 Furnish welding electrodes.

11. Mechanical equipment erection

1.0 Scope

The Contractor shall furnish all supervision, labor, equipment, tools, precision instruments, supplies, new materials, unload, store, protect, remove from storage, transport, rig, install, final align, lubricate, service, rotate, check out and make ready for operation equipment furnished by others as outlined in enumerated systems.

Scope of work shall include, but not necessarily be limited to the setting of equipment in the following systems:

Main Stream, Main Feedwater, Auxiliary Feedwater, Auxiliary Boiler, Diesel Generator, Diesel Fuel Oil Storage and Transfer, BOP Service Water, Nitrogen Gas, Demineralized Water Makeup, Condensate Storage, Moisture Separator Reheater Drain, H2 and CO2 Supply, Feedwater Heater Drain, Chilled Water, Primary Gas, Primary Water, Vents and Drains, Component Cooling, Instrument Air, Hydrogen Control, Chemical Addition. (Figure 17)

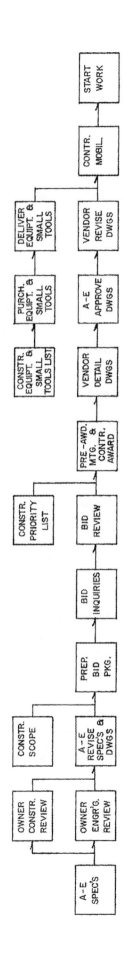

FIGURE #17

CONTRACT   PACKAGE
MECHANICAL   EQUIPMENT   ERECTION

2.0 Work By Contractor

    2.1   Unload, store, protect, remove from storage, set, level, align, shim, dowel and grout disassembled pumps, hydraulic couplings, (other than HVAC), auxiliary boilers and associated equipment, diesel generators and associated equipment, all equipment in Intake Structure, laboratory mechanical equipment and kitchen and laundry equipment.

    2.2   Unload, handle, set and level all floor mounted cranes, permanent jibs, and hoists including rails and monorails and grouting where required.

    2.3   Install cranes and monorails other than overhead cranes.

    2.4   Erect all hangers, supports and base plates including seismic and/or jet force restraints for equipment.

    2.5   Maintenance of equipment in storage, including protection as recommended by equipment manufacturer.

    2.6   All surveying and layout from project survey control points established by Owner.

    2.7   Power extension from load centers, compressed air, bottled gas and air, sanitary facilities including maintenance thereof until such time as construction facilities are in service, and drinking and construction water from designated onsite source.

3.0 Construction Procedures and QA/QC Requirements.

    3.1   The Contractor shall comply and conform to Quality Assurance requirements as delineated in the specifications and referenced codes and standards.

    3.2   The Contractor shall submit for approval his complete Quality Assurance Program which shall be in conformance with Quality Assurance Criteria for Fossil Fuel Power Plants.

    3.3   Contractors shall submit detailed Quality Assurance Control procedures as required by the Engineer's specification.

    3.4   Contractor shall initiate construction installation procedures in detail for all work within his scope. The procedures shall include but not be limited to the following: Erection of materials in conformance with specifications, drawings, codes, welding procedures including operator and process welding procedures, certified data sheets of welding procedures, stress relieving procedures including operator and process welding procedures, certified data sheets of welding procedures, stress relieving procedures, erection sequence and shop fabrication procedures and controls, quality control checklist, calibration of test equipment and tools, alignment devices and procedures for maintenance of alignment and erection tolerances and calibration field precision instruments.

    3.5   Construction procedures shall conform to applicable codes and the Engineer's specifications. All construction installation procedures shall be reviewed by the Construction Managers; work shall not start until procedures have been reviewed and approved in writing. A deviation from approved procedures will require an addendum which must be approved in writing by the Construction Manager prior to resuming the specific work in question.

3.6 The Contractor shall furnish materials and perform all work in accordance with specifications, drawings, including notes thereon, referenced specifications, all applicable codes and procedures, and in conformance with all local, state and federal codes and regulations. Submittals of materials and drawings shall be specified elsewhere in the contract documents.

4.0 Work Not Included
    4.1   Installation of elevators.
    4.2   Erection of field fabricated tanks.
    4.3   Installation of HVAC and associated equipment.
    4.4   Installation of Turbine-Generator, condenser and auxiliary equipment.
    4.5   Equipment foundations and embedded steel.
    4.6   Setting of separate electrical motors, switchgear and panels.
    4.7   Electrical, piping, instrumentation and insulation.
    4.8   Furnishing of all permanent equipment.
    4.9   Installation of boiler plant equipment.
    4.10 Furnish welding electrodes.

12. FIRE SPECIALTIES
1.0 Scope

The Contractor shall furnish all supervision, labor, services, new materials, tools instruments, equipment to install the fixed water spray deluge systems, stand pipe systems, fixed detection devices, and portable fire extinguishers and all associated fire specialties specified by the Engineer; receive, unload, store, protect, remove from storage, transport, rig, install, checkout, test and make ready for operation the entire fire protection systems in the permanent building except the outside yard main fire loop, and its associated equipment including fire water storage tanks, fire pumps, jockey pumps and control equipment, all of which will have been installed by others. (Figure 18)

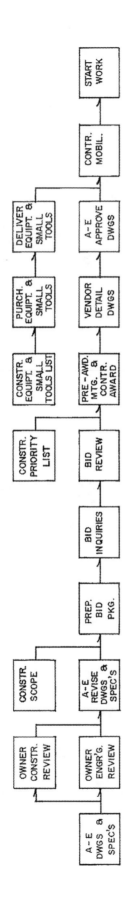

FIGURE #18

CONTRACT PACKAGE
FIRE SPECIALTIES

2.0 Work By Contractor

    2.1 The Contractor shall be responsible for furnishing, receiving, and verifying and recording all material documentation required by all applicable codes including but not limited to National Fire Protection Association Codes (NFPA), Part 1910, "Occupational Safety and Health Standards", and codes and regulations of the state and Quality Assurance/Quality Control standards described elsewhere in Engineer's specification.

    2.2 The Contractor shall perform and/or provide test laboratory services to complete all nondestructive tests in accordance with applicable codes, standards, and QA/QC procedures.

    2.3 Contractor shall furnish and erect all piping as enumerated by systems, including valves, piping specialties, engineered hanger systems and supplemental supporting steel for hanger systems.

    2.4 The Contractor shall complete each system fully, clean, hydrostatically test at 15 per cent above normal operating pressure, adjust, proof flush and make ready for pre-operational testing the major systems including the following:

        2.4.1 Water supply system (the outside closed fire loop, fire water storage tanks, pumps and structural scope of work is installed in the contract Package, and it is not included in this Contractor's scope of work; however final testing will be required for the entire systems in this contract as well as in Contract number); however, the Contractor shall furnish and install valves and branch lines from fire loop into each building shown on drawings and specified by Engineer.

        2.4.2 Yard protection system is installed under Contract Package number, and not included in this scope.

        2.4.3 Fixed water spray deluge protection shall be provided and shall be furnished and installed for each of the following:

            2.4.3.1 Generator step-up transformers.

            2.4.3.2 Unit Auxiliary transformers.

            2.4.3.3 Reserve auxiliary transformers.

            2.4.3.4 Standby reserve auxiliary transformers.

            2.4.3.5 Station auxiliary transformer.

            2.4.3.6 Hydrogen seal oil units.

            2.4.3.7 Turbine oil reservoirs.

            2.4.3.8 Lube oil conditioner.

        2.4.4 The Contractor shall furnish and locate throughout the site as specified by the Engineer and shown on drawings, portable fire extinguishers of the type to be used against small first and best suited to extinguish the combustible materials present, without presenting a hazard to personnel from toxic fumes or electric shock; the extinguishers are to be conveniently located and conspicuously marked.

        2.4.5 Testing and inspection of the entire fire protection system shall be performed by the Contractor even though part of the system may have been previously installed and tested by others. The fire pumps and systems shall be tested and inspected as specified by the Engineer and in general conformance with the requirements of authorities, fire underwriters having jurisdiction and recommendation of nationally recognized fire protection association standards.

2.4.6 All Safety devices shall be checked, tested, and set for proper and safe relieving pressures.

2.4.7 The Contractor shall assist in startup operations as specified.

2.5 Survey and layout from project control points established by the Owner.

2.6 Power extension from load centers, compressed air, bottled gas, welding equipment, and drinking and construction water from designated on-site source.

3.0 Construction Procedures and QA/QC Requirements

3.1 The Contractor shall comply and conform to Quality Assurance requirements as delineated in the specifications and referenced codes and standards.

3.2 The Contractor shall submit for approval his complete Quality Assurance Program which shall be in conformance with the Quality Assurance criteria for Fossil Power Plants.

3.3 Contractor shall submit detailed Quality Assurance Control procedures as required by the Engineer's specification.

3.4 Contractor shall initiate construction installation procedures in detail for all work within his scope. The procedures shall include but not be limited to the following; erection of all materials in conformance with specifications, drawings, codes, welding procedures when required, including operator and process welding procedures, certified data sheets of welding procedures, stress relieving procedures, erection sequence and shop fabrication procedures and controls, Quality control checklist, calibration of test equipment and tools, alignment devices and procedures for maintenance of alignment and erection of tolerances and calibration field precision instruments.

3.5 Construction procedures shall conform to applicable codes and the Engineer's specifications. All construction installation procedures shall be reviewed by the Construction Managers; work shall not start until procedures have been reviewed and approved in writing. A deviation from approved procedures will require an addendum which must be approved in writing by the Construction Manager prior to resuming the specific work in question.

3.6 The Contractor shall furnish materials and perform all work in accordance with specifications, drawings, including notes thereon, referenced specifications, all applicable codes and procedures, and in conformance with all local, state and federal codes and regulations. Submittals of materials and drawings shall be as specified elsewhere in the contract documents.

4.0 Work Not Included.

4.1 Site clearing, general excavation and grading.

4.2 Fire protection piping in temporary buildings.

4.3 Outside piping fire protection loop.

4.4 Foundations for fire water tank and pump house.

4.5 Erection of two 30,000 gallon fire water storage tanks.

4.6 Control equipment for fire pump house installation.

4.7 Backfilling and bedding trenches.

4.8 Embedded items.

4.9 Potable water pumps and piping system.

4.10 Long electrical conduit and wiring. Wiring in cable trays and long runs to control room for alarm systems and power supplied by others.

4.11 Furnish welding electrodes.

13. HVAC INSTALLATION

1.0 Scope

The Contractor shall furnish all supervision, labor, new material, tools and equipment necessary to design, detail, fabricate, deliver as required; and to purchase, deliver, unload, store, protect and/or transport, install and test the heating, ventilating and air conditioning equipment as specified; unload, protect, erect, test, place in service and balance the HVAC System; to install all prepurchased, Owner furnished HVAC equipment and components. (Figure 19)

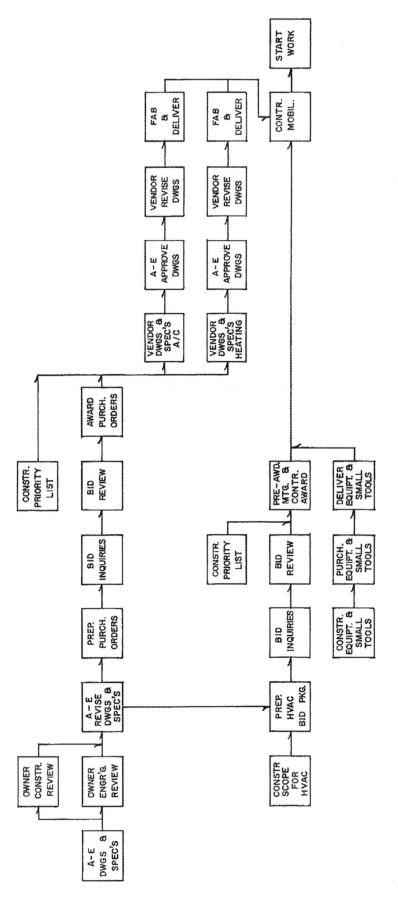

FIGURE #19

CONTRACT PACKAGE
HVAC INSTALLATION

2.0 Work By Contractor.

The work shall include but not be limited to the fabrication and/or purchase, installation, test and preparation of placing in service the following:

    2.1   Supply and return air fans as specified.

    2.2   Air handling units.

    2.3   Water chillers.

    2.4   Cooling and heating coils.

    2.5   Fire and control dampers.

    2.6   Condenser, spray and chilled water pumps integral with HVAC System.

    2.7   Check and butterfly valves which are part of HVAC System.

    2.8   Intake and exhaust louvers.

    2.9   Vent Duct (stack).

    2.10 Humidifiers.

    2.11 Roll-a-matic and roughing filters and installation only of HEPA and charcoal filters.

    2.12 Evaporate coolers.

    2.13 Compressor condensing units.

    2.14 Roof vent fans.

    2.15 Exhaust hoods.

    2.16 Kitchen and toilet exhaust fans.

    2.17 Ductwork, duct hangers and supports associated with foregoing systems.

    2.18 Provide all equipment necessary to test and balance the HVAC Systems as required.

    2.19 Furnish, install, calibrate and test all pneumatic instrumentation which is an integral part of the HVAC System; and furnish and install all local controls including local electrical work. (Specify special requirements for Class 1 electrical areas).

    2.20 Install, test and place in service all pre purchased equipment supplied by Owner and itemized in Engineer's specifications.

    2.21 Supply test procedures and operating and maintenance manuals including parts list.

    2.22 Insulate HVAC ductwork and equipment as required.

    2.23 Vibration eliminators.

    2.24 All surveying and layout from project survey control points established by Owner.

    2.25 All temporary field fabrication facilities, power extension from load centers, compressed air, bottled gas and air, sanitary facilities including maintenance thereof until such time as construction facilities are in service and drinking and construction water from designated onsite source.

3.0 Work Not Included

    3.1   Concrete work.

    3.2   Piping external to the HVAC System, including steam unit heaters.

    3.3   General painting.

3.4 Structural steel supporting systems.

3.5 Remote electrical instrumentation and long conduit and wiring.

3.6 Embedded anchor bolts.

3.7 Furnishing of HEPA and charcoal filters and other Category 1 items.

3.8 Temporary office and changehouse.

3.9 Furnish and install unit heaters.

3.10 Furnish welding electrodes.

14. ELECTRICAL INSTALLATION SWITCHYARD AND RELAY EQUIPMENT

1.0 Scope

The Contractor shall provide supervision, labor and tools (under $600.00 each value) to install complete the permanent electrical work for the switching substation, including installing underground duct, electrical manholes, conduit, cable tray, raceways, except embedded materials; unload (except transformers), store, protect, transport, erect and install, test and place in service all pre purchased material for the switching substation, including but not limited to switchgear, bus supporting structures and buses, relay panes, and cabinets in substation relay room and pull and terminated cable from substation to relay room. This scope includes step up transformers and unit transformers equipment installation. (Figure 20)

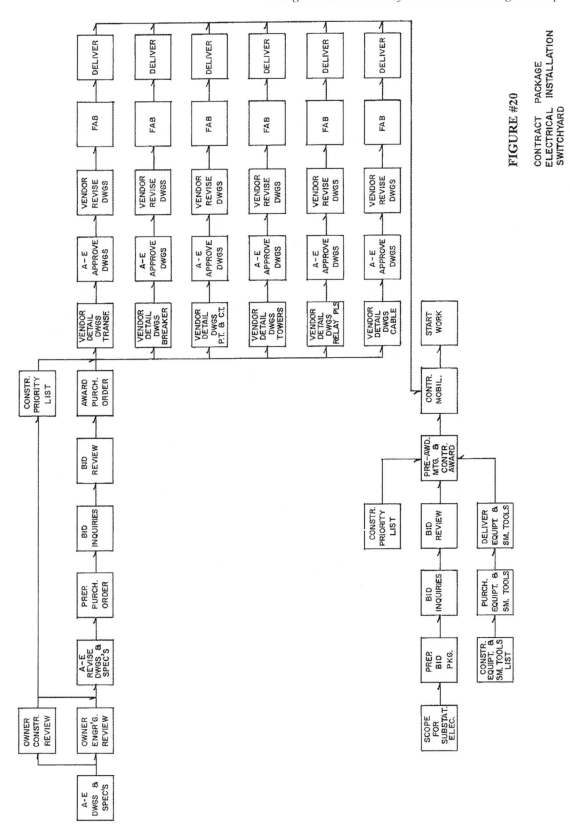

FIGURE #20

CONTRACT PACKAGE
ELECTRICAL INSTALLATION
SWITCHYARD

2.0 Work By Contractor.

The Contractor shall install, test and place in service equipment for the switchyard substation; detailed requirements will be provided to Contractor for performance of the work.

3.0 Construction Procedures and QA/QC Requirements.

    1.1 The Contractor shall comply and conform to Quality Assurance requirements as delineated in the specifications and referenced codes and standards.

    1.2 Contractor shall submit detailed Quality Assurance and Control procedures as required by the Engineer's specifications.

    1.3 Contractor shall initiate construction installation procedures in detail for all work within his scope. The procedures shall include but not be limited to the following: erection of materials for switchyard substation in conformance with specifications, drawings, codes, welding procedures including operator and process welding procedures, certified data sheets of welding procedures, stress relieving procedures, erection sequence and procedures and controls. Quality Control checklist, calibration of test equipment and tools, alignment devices and procedures for maintenance of alignment and erection tolerances and calibration field precision instruments.

    1.4 Construction procedures shall conform to applicable codes and the Engineer's specifications. All construction installation procedures shall be reviewed by the construction Managers; work shall not start until procedures have been reviewed and approved in writing by the Construction Managers prior to resuming the specific work in question.

    1.5 The Contractor shall furnish materials and perform all work in accordance with specifications, drawings, including notes thereon, referenced specifications, all applicable codes and procedures and in conformance with all local, state and federal codes and regulations. Submittals of materials and drawings shall be as specified elsewhere in the contract documents.

1.3 Work Not Included

    3.1 Structural, mechanical and piping (except for transformers).

    3.2 Construction of transformer foundations and fire walls

    3.3 Switchyard foundations.

    3.4 Construction of electrical tunnels, manholes, concrete encasement for duct banks.

    3.5 Electrical embedments.

    3.6 Temporary systems.

    3.7 Furnish welding electrodes.

15. ELECTRICAL INSTALLATION-PERMANENT

1.0 Scope

The Contractor shall provide all supervision, labor, tools (under $600.00 each value) to install complete the permanent electrical power system including furnishing and installation of all underground ducts, electrical manhole and vaults, conduit, cable tray, raceways, except embedded materials; install and test complete lighting systems, including lighting panes; unload, store, protect, transport, install and test, place in service pre purchased items furnished by Owner, including but not limited to switchgear, motor control centers, electrical control panels, electrical racks, computer equipment, communication equipment, closed circuit TV equipment, miscellaneous electrical cabinets and all motors shipped separately, together with all associated power and control cables, bus, grounding, installation and testing of all cable, terminations, fireproofing, electrical installation power supply to all overhead cranes and monorails. Install all long wiring and remote controls for HVAC Systems. (Figures 21 & 22)

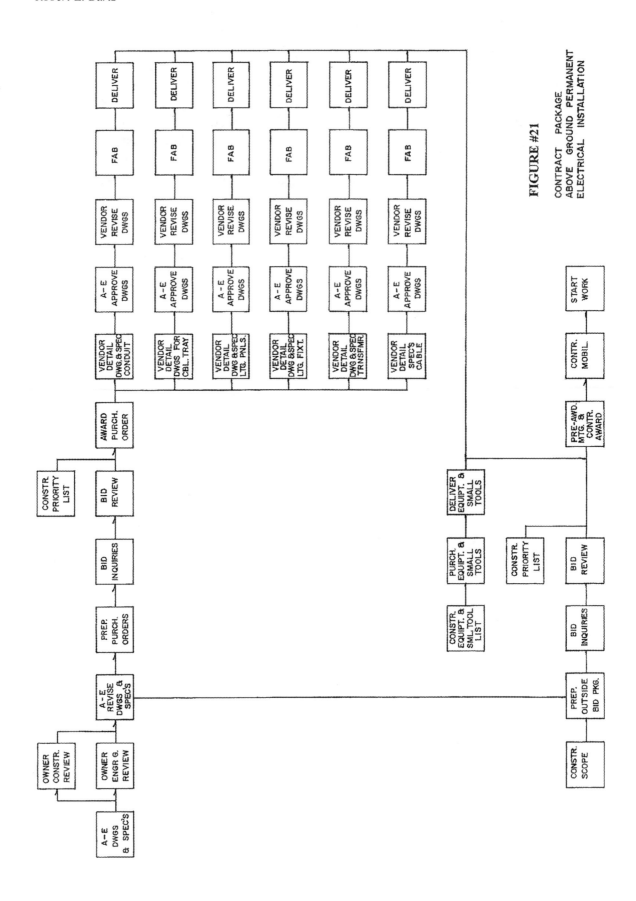

FIGURE #21

CONTRACT PACKAGE
ABOVE GROUND PERMANENT
ELECTRICAL INSTALLATION

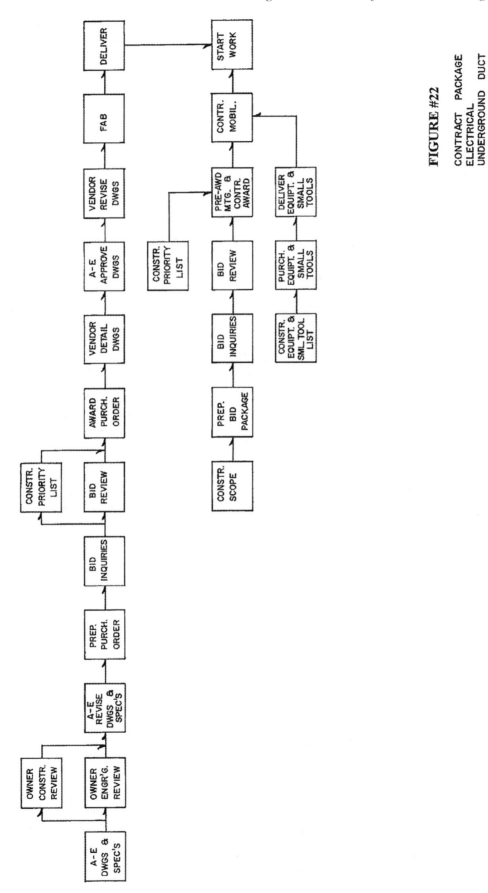

FIGURE #22

CONTRACT PACKAGE
ELECTRICAL
UNDERGROUND DUCT

2.0 Work By Contractor

    2.1 The Electrical Contractor will be required to install and test equipment for the following systems;

        a. Lighting system fixtures, indoor and outdoor.
        b. Lighting system wire and cable.
        c. Lighting system transformers.
        d. Lighting system distribution panes.

    2.2 Detailed requirements will be provided to the Contractor for the performance of work in the following areas;

        a. Cable, conduit, tray and equipment marking.
        b. Cable fire proofing in manholes, floor and wall openings.
        c. Cable installation including maximum pull tensions as specified megger and hi-pot requirements.
        d. Cable termination and splicing requirements in accordance with manufacturer's recommendations. This will include details on stress cones and potheads, etc., as well as special termination requirements for coaxial and triaxial and thermocouple wires.
        e. Use of the computer produced cable pull slips.
        f. Information feedback requirements for input to the computerized construction main power control program.
        g. Tray hanging requirements and conduit installation requirements.
        h. Grounding requirements, i.e. cad welding, ground strips over shields.
        i. Installation and testing of electrical penetrations including welding, if required.
        j. Installation and testing of pre purchased equipment such as switchgear, motor control centers, batteries and chargers, etc., and storage instructions for pre purchased equipment.
        k. Plant security system, closed circuit TV.
        l. Plant security system, intruder protection system, if required.

    2.3 Install power supply wiring and collectors for all cranes including Containment, General Service, Intake and Turbine Generator Buildings. All wiring and controls for all monorails and job cranes.

    2.4 Install all long wiring to control room conduit, tray and electrical remote controls for HVAC and fire protection system.

    2.5 Installation of all long wire and cable for electrical contract.

    2.6 Control room ceiling installation complete.

    2.7 Maintenance of electrical material onsite and/or in storage and periodic testing, such as rotation and meggering, etc.

    2.8 All surveying and layout from project survey control points established by Owner.

    2.9 Power extension from load centers, compressed air, bottled gas and air, sanitary facilities including maintenance thereof until construction facilities are available and drinking and construction water from designated onsite source.

3.0 Construction Procedures and QA/QC Requirements

    3.1 The Contractor shall comply and conform to Quality Assurance requirements as delineated in the specifications and referenced codes and standards.

    3.2 The Contractor shall submit for approval his complete Quality Assurance Program which shall be in conformance with the Quality Assurance Criteria for Fossil Power Plants.

    3.3 Contractor shall submit detailed Quality Assurance control procedures as required by the Engineer's specification.

    3.4 Contractor shall initiate construction installation procedures in detail for all work within his scope. The procedures shall include but not be limited to the following: erection and installation of materials for electrical work in conformance with specifications, drawings, codes, welding procedures including operator and process welding procedures, quality control checklist, calibration of test equipment and tools, alignment devices and procedures for maintenance of alignment and erection tolerances and calibration field precision instruments.

    3.5 Construction procedures shall conform to applicable codes and the engineer's specifications. All construction installation procedures shall be reviewed by the Construction Managers; work shall not start until procedures have been reviewed and approved in writing. A deviation from approved procedures will require an addendum which must be approved in writing by the Construction Managers prior to resuming the specific work in question.

    3.6 The Contractor shall furnish materials and perform all work in accordance with specifications, drawings, including notes thereon, referenced specifications, all applicable codes and procedures, and in conformance with all local, state and federal codes and regulations. Submittals of materials and drawings shall be as specified elsewhere in the contract documents.

4.0 Work Not Included.

    4.1 Structural, mechanical and piping work.

    4.2 Construction of transformer foundations and firewall.

    4.3 Switchyard foundations and switchyard substation work.

    4.4 Embedments for electrical work.

    4.5 Construction of electrical tunnels, manholes and concrete encasement for duct banks.

    4.6 Temporary power system including maintenance.

    4.7 Furnish welding electrodes.

16. INSTRUMENTATION.

1.0 Scope

The Contractor shall furnish all supervision, labor services, consumables, supplies, tools (under $600.00 each value) and accessories to install all station instrumentation, except that instrumentation associated with other Contractor installed equipment or systems, including but not limited to instrumentation furnished by the Steam Supply System vendor and the Owner as fully described and specified by the Engineer. (Figure 23)

Robert E. Bartz

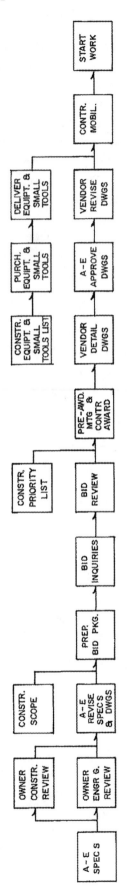

FIGURE #23

CONTRACT PACKAGE
INSTRUMENT INSTALLATION

2.0 Work By Contractor.

2.1 The Instrumentation Contractor shall be responsible for receiving and verifying and recording by applicable codes, standards, and Quality Assurance/ Quality Control standards described elsewhere in the Engineer's specification.

2.2 The Contractor shall perform and/or provide all nondestructive tests required and document all results of tests in accordance with applicable codes, standards, specifications. QA/QC procedures.

2.3 The Contractor shall receive, protect, store and if required in Engineer's specification, store in controlled atmospheric conditions, calibrate, bench check and prior to startup loop check all instrumentation installed.

2.4 The Contractor shall install all pneumatic instrumentation, including tubing, pipe, valves and specialties for all systems.

2.5 All pneumatic or combined pneumatic-electrical systems including panels and racks shall be installed by this Contractor.

2.6 The Contractor shall install under directions of the Engineer's specification and the manufacturer's Service Engineer Supervisors, the station computer system as specified.

2.7 The Contractor shall install, test and loop check test all instrumentation, pneumatic as well as electrical or combined pneumatic-electrical instrumentation systems in the control room and at remote station locations.

2.8 The Contractor shall be responsible for protection of all installed instruments, gauges, panels, cabinets, control panels, racks, etc., until test and startup operation begins.

2.9 The Contractor shall accept all electrical terminations made by the Prime Electrical Contractor as being installed properly and correctly as indicated on the drawings and specified by the Engineer. In the event that the terminations have been incorrectly made or the manufacturer's fabrication and wiring is in error, the Instrumentation Contractor shall immediately, in writing, advise the Construction Manager and request immediate remedial action. At the Construction Manager's option, the Instrumentation Contractor may be directed to make all required field corrections to the terminations and full document all changes required in accordance with established detailed Quality Assurance/Quality Control Procedures.

2.10 The Contractor is responsible only for the complete loop checking out sequence required or specified by the Engineer for the instrumentation systems enumerated.

2.11 All shop fabricated panels and racks materials furnished are specified by drawings and Engineer's specifications.

2.12 The Contractor shall erect all instrumentation piping as enumerated by systems, including all valves, piping specialties, engineered hanger systems and field fabricated hanger systems.

2.13 the erection of instrumentation piping systems shall include but not be limited to handling, protection, alignment, fit-up with alignment templates and/or devises if required, welding, stress relieving, if required, provide labor to hydrostatically test and flush completed systems and disposal of water from tested systems. Erect clean test rooms and provide clean room conditions where specified for equipment. Some isometric piping sketches will be forwarded to Contractor' remaining isometrics for all piping systems shall be prepared by the contractor and forwarded to Engineer as specified.

2.14 Contractor shall erect all pipe hangers and supplemental support steel for hangers, seismic and/or jet force restraints, supports, valves, appurtenances and pipe specialties furnished and fabricated by others as enumerated by system.

2.15 Contractor shall fabricate and erect all small diameter instrumentation piping and tubing including preparations of isometric drawings.

2.16 The Contractor shall submit to Engineer for approval of all welding procedures and certified test laboratory data sheets for each and every welding procedure used. Contractor must qualify all welders to the specified approved procedures as required by Engineer's specification and ASME Code Section III and IX and other applicable section of the ASME Codes, or standards referenced.

2.17 Contractor shall provide and maintain a map and weld record of each and every weld for each piping system, showing location of weld, weld identifying number, welder(s) number and name, preheat data stress relieving, post heat data and charts, inspection data sheet for each weld and/or passes to complete weld, repairs and repair procedures used, physical and chemical analyses of weld metal.

2.18 Contractor shall qualify welders to applicable welding procedures.

2.19 Contractor shall provide for Engineer's review and approval procedures which shall include end preparation and tit-up and alignment methods and/or devices used to meet code tolerances as specified.

2.20 The Contractor shall complete each system, fully clean, test, adjust and set hangers in cold and/or hot position prior to turnover for preoperational testing.

2.21 Contractor shall assist in startup operation as specified.

2.22 All surveying and layout from project survey control points established by Owner.

2.23 Power extension from load centers, compressed air, bottled gas and air, drinking and construction water from designated onsite source; and connections to and from source of demineralized water for test purposes and disposal of demineralized water upon completion of specified tests.

3.0 Construction Procedures and QA/QC Requirements

3.1 The Contractor shall comply and conform to quality Assurance requirements as delineated in the specifications and referenced codes and standards.

3.2 The Contractor shall submit for approval his complete Quality Assurance Program which shall be in conformance with the Quality Assurance Criteria for Fossil Power Plants.

3.3 Contractor shall submit detailing Quality Assurance control procedures as required by the Engineer's specifications.

3.4 Contractor shall initiate construction installation procedures in detail for all work within his scope. The procedure shall include but not be limited to the following: erection and/or installation of materials in conformance with specifications, drawings, codes, welding procedures including operator and process welding procedures, certified data sheets of welding procedures, stress relieving procedures, erection sequence and shop fabrication procedures and controls, Quality Control checklist, calibration field precision instruments.

3.5 Construction procedures shall conform to applicable codes and the Engineer's specifications. All construction installation procedures shall be reviewed by the Construction Managers; work shall not start until procedures have been reviewed and approved in writing. A deviation from approved procedures will require an addendum which must be approved in writing by the Construction Managers prior to resuming the specific work in question.

3.6 The Contractor shall furnish materials and perform all work in accordance with specifications, drawings, including notes thereon, referenced specifications, all applicable codes and procedures, and in conformance with all local, state and federal codes and regulations. Submittals of materials and drawings shall be as specified elsewhere in the contract documents.

3.7 The Contractor shall furnish the Engineer certified copies of current certificates of authorization for use of the following ASME stamps, i.e., "N", "NPT", "PP", and other code symbol stamps for execution of his scope of work under the ASME code sections for the project.

4.0 Work Not Included.

4.1 Furnishing equipment for any instrumentation systems enumerated and/or included instruments, gauges, flow meters, orifices, transducers, sensors or any element of a system.

4.2 Furnishing pipe, tubing, fittings, piping specialties valves, and valve operators either motor or pneumatically operated.

4.3 engineered hanger systems.

4.4 Miscellaneous steel for supports, racks, trays or conduits, cabinets, panels and/or plate for field fabricated panels.

4.5 All electrical wire of whatever size or insulation requirements.

4.6 Lugs, connectors, and/or special connections between and/or for electrical-pneumatic combination equipment.

4.7 Long line electrical circuit pulls between termination points, including dropouts from trays, to equipment.

4.8 Multiplex conductors of any description.

4.9 Any special instrumentation wiring and/or engineering required for noise protections.

4.10 Noise protective devices and/or engineering required for noise protection.

4.11 Special shielding and/or shielded cabled conductors.

4.12 Survey control points.

4.13 Temporary power distribution system, temporary facilities, electrical work and maintenance of temporary electrical facilities.

4.14 Electrical work, electrical power wiring of equipment and electrical checking and testing of work installed by others unless specifically specified by Engineer's specifications.

4.15 Manufacturer's service and/or test Engineers.

4.16 Procedural and/or system description manuals of work installed.

4.17 Furnishing or installation of instrumentation for HVAC system.

4.18 Furnish welding electrodes.

17. TURBINE GENERATOR INSTALLATION

1.0 Scope

The Contractor shall furnish all supervision, labor, equipment, tools (under $600.00 each value) instruments, supplies, materials to unload, store, protect, transport, rig, set, shim, align, level and dowel, the Turbine Generator and auxiliaries as delineated and specified. (Figure 24)

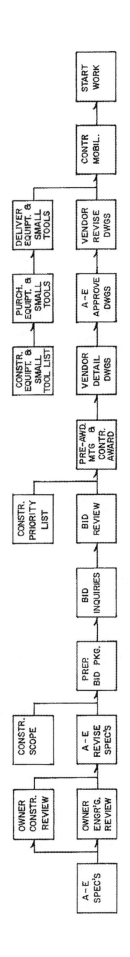

FIGURE #24

CONTRACT PACKAGE
TURBINE GENERATOR
INSTALLATION

2.0 Work By Contractor.

2.1 The Contractor shall unload, handle, set, shim, level, align and grout all turbine, generator, exciter soleplates and sub soleplates and lagging supports.

2.2 The Contractor shall unload, store and protect, rig, install, level and align generator rotor and stator, governor and exciter and all turbine parts and accessories, including but not limited to, all steam, water, oil, gland seal, drain, hydraulic CO2 and H2 piping systems and other supporting piping systems, including equipment, valves, hangers, strainers and instrumentation integral with the equipment and auxiliaries all furnished by the equipment manufacturer and to limits shown on Engineer's drawings and as specified.

2.3 The Contractor shall install all piping, hangers, valves and other piping specialties, including installation of all heat retention lagging and pipe insulation required and specified by the Engineer.

2.4 The Contractor shall be responsible for receiving and verifying and recording all material documentation as required by all applicable codes, standards and Quality Assurance/Quality Control standards described elsewhere in Engineer's specifications.

2.5 The Contractor shall perform and/or provide test laboratory services to complete all non destructive tests required and document to results of all tests in accordance with applicable codes, specifications, standards and QA/QC procedures.

2.6 The Contractor shall erect all piping and enumerated by systems including all valves, piping specialties, engineered hanger systems and filed fabricated hanger systems.

2.7 The erection of piping systems shall include but not be limited to handling, protecting, alignment, fit-up with alignment templates and/or devices if required, welding, stress relieving, cleanup and prepare completed welds for in service inspection, if required, provide labor to hydrostatically test and flush completed systems and disposal of water from tested systems. Provide labor for acid cleaning and flushing of certain piping system.

2.8 Some isometrics piping sketches will be forwarded to Contractor; remaining isometrics for all piping systems shall be prepared by the Contractor and forwarded to Engineer as specifies.

2.9 Contractor shall erect all pipe hangers and supplemental support steel for hangers, seismic and/or jet force restraints, supports, valves, appurtenances and pipe specialties furnished and fabricated by others as enumerated by system.

2.10 Contractor shall fabricate and erect all small diameter piping, including preparations of isometric drawings.

2.11 The Contractor shall submit to Engineer for approval all welding procedures and certified test laboratory data sheets for each and every welding procedure use. Contractor must qualify all welders to the specified approved procedures as required by Engineer's specifications and ASME Code Section IX and other applicable sections of the ASME Codes or standards referenced.

2.12 Contractor shall provide and maintain a map and weld record of each and every weld for each piping system, showing location of weld, weld identifying number, welder(s) number and name, preheat data stress relieving post heat data and charts inspection data sheet for each weld and/ or passes to complete weld, repairs and repair procedures used, physical and chemical analyses of weld metal.

2.13 Contractor shall qualify welders to be used on connections to turbine supplied pipe to those procedures approved and furnished by the T-G Manufacturer's Engineering Department for use on this project only.

2.14 Contractor shall provide for Engineer's review and approval procedures which shall include preparation and fit-up and alignment methods and/or devises used to meet code tolerances as specified.

2.15 Contractor shall unload and set Turbine Generator manufacturer's supplied control panels and supervisory instrument panels and install all electrical interconnections supplied by manufacturer including conduit, brackets integral with these electrical appurtenances and shall connect to terminal blocks.

2.16 The Contractor shall complete each system fully, clean, test, adjust and set hangers in cold and/or hot position prior to turnover for pre operational testing.

2.17 The Contractor shall unload initial turbine oil supplied by Owner and fill turbine oil reservoir for oil flush. Flush system as specified and filter used oil and /or refill system with new oil batch supplied by Owner.

2.18 The Contractor shall be responsible for cleaning, flushing, testing, start up assistance, and maintenance in accordance with manufacturer's recommendations.

2.19 The Contractor shall be responsible at all times to receive and follow technical direction and assistance from the manufacturer's qualified erection Engineers for the following:

2.19.1 Setting and grouting of equipment soleplates and mounting plates.

2.19.2 Unloading and transferring equipment and materials to temporary field storage and/or to final location.

2.19.3 Assembly, installation and erection of all equipment.

2.19.4 Inspection of assembly, alignment, cleanliness of all parts, components and sub-assemblies.

2.19.5 Starting and testing of equipment.

2.20 Contractor shall assist in start-up operation as specified.

2.21 All surveying and layout from project survey control points established by Owner.

2.22 All temporary facilities including offices, changehouses, warehouses and shops as required; power extension from load centers, compressed air, bottled gas and air, sanitary facilities including maintenance thereof, and drinking and construction water from designated onsite source.

3.0 Construction Procedures and QA/QC Requirements.

    3.1 The Contractor shall comply and conform to Quality Assurance requirements as delineated in the specifications and referenced codes and standards.

    3.2 The Contractor shall submit for approval his complete Quality Assurance Program which shall be in conformance with the Quality Assurance Program which shall be in conformance with the Quality Assurance Criteria for Fossil Power Plants.

    3.3 Contractor shall submit detailed Quality Assurance control procedures as required by the Engineer's specifications.

    3.4 Contractor shall initiate construction installation procedures in detail for all work within his scope. The procedures shall include but not be limited to the following: erection of materials in conformance with specifications, drawings, codes, welding procedures including operator and process welding procedures, certified data sheets of welding procedures, stress relieving procedures, erection sequence and shop fabrication procedures and controls, quality control check list, calibration of test equipment and tools, alignment devices and procedures for maintenance of alignment and erection tolerances and calibration field precision instruments.

    3.5 Construction procedures shall conform to applicable codes and the Engineer's specifications. All construction installation procedures shall be reviewed by the Construction Managers; work shall not start until procedures have been reviewed and approved in writing.

    3.6 A deviation from approved procedures will require in addendum which must be approved in writing by the Construction Managers prior to resuming the specific work in question.

    3.7 The Contractor shall furnish materials and perform all work in accordance with specifications, drawings, including notes thereon, references specifications, all applicable codes and procedures and in conformance with all local, state and federal codes and regulations. Submittals of materials and drawings shall be as specified elsewhere in the contract documents.

4.0 Work Not Included.

    4.1 Furnish Turbine Generator and auxiliary equipment including pipe, electrical and instrumentation.

    4.2 Install external cable and connections to terminal blocks and exciter, static rectifier and associated excitation and voltage regulation switchgear.

    4.3 Installation of piping, electrical and instrumentation external to equipment and material supplied by T-G manufacturer.

    4.4 Installation of foundation and anchor bolts.

    4.5 Installation of fire protection system.

    4.6 Technical direction by T-G manufacturer.

    4.7 Furnishing of major mechanical, electrical and instrumentation equipment.

    4.8 Furnish welding electrodes.

18. ELEVATORS

1.0 Scope

Contractor shall design, detail and furnish all supervision, labor, new materials, tools (under $600.00 each value) and equipment to fabricate, deliver, unload, store, protect and/or transport, erect and test all freight and passenger elevators as indicated on the drawings for each unit; maintenance of same shall be included for the duration of the construction period for each unit. (Figure 25)

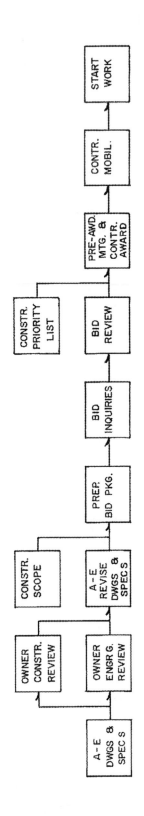

FIGURE #25

CONTRACT PACKAGE
ELEVATORS

2.0 Work By Contractor

    2.1 Design, furnish and erect elevators including hoisting machinery, counterweights, electrical and mechanical control equipment, cab and doors, guide rails, frames, sills, wiring, trim, hardware and other associated appurtenances to provide a complete system.

    2.2 Lubricate and test equipment acceptable to the state licensing authority prior to acceptance.

    2.3 Contractor shall furnish and install temporary liner protection on walls, floors and ceiling designed to take construction abuse for about one and one half years for each scheduled construction period for each unit.

    2.4 Provide compartment and internal wiring for telephone connection.

    2.5 Install all safety devices, interlocks and guards as required by state and federal laws.

    2.6 Provide maintenance on elevators as enumerated in the contract documents for a period of approximately one and one half years from the start of contract work in each scheduled construction period for each unit.

    2.7 Furnish placement drawings for embedments.

    2.8 All surveying and layout from project survey control points established by Owner.

    2.9 All temporary facilities including offices, changehouses, warehouses and shops as required; power extension from load centers, compressed air, bottled gas and air, sanitary facilities including maintenance thereof, and drinking and construction water from designated on site source.

3.0 Construction Procedures and QA/QC Requirements.

    3.1 The Contractor shall comply and conform to Quality Assurance requirements as delineated in the specifications and referenced codes and standards.

    3.2 The contractor shall submit for approval his complete Quality Assurance Program which shall be in conformance with Quality Assurance Criteria for Fossil Fuel Power Plants.

    3.3 Contractor shall submit detailed Quality Assurance control procedures as required by the Engineer's specification.

    3.4 Contractor shall initiate construction installation procedures in detail for all work within his scope. The procedures shall include but not be limited to the following; erection of materials in conformance with specifications, drawings, codes, quality control checklist, calibration of test equipment and tools, alignment devices and procedures for ;maintenance of alignment and erection tolerances and calibration field precision instruments.

    3.5 Construction procedures shall conform to applicable codes and the Engineer's specifications. All construction installation procedures shall be reviewed by the Construction Managers; work shall not start until procedures have been reviewed and approved in writing. A deviation from approved procedures will require an addendum which must be approved in writing by the Construction Managers prior to resuming the specific work in question.

    3.6 The Contractor shall furnish materials and perform all work in accordance with specifications, drawings, including notes thereon, referenced specifications, all applicable codes and procedures, are in conformance with all local, state and federal codes and regulations. Submittals of materials and drawings shall be as specified elsewhere in the contract documents.

4.0 Work Not Included.

    4.1 Construction of elevator shafts including embedments for rail attachments and machinery room, concrete, masonry, embedded iron, anchor bolts, structural steel, etc.

    4.2 Electrical power supply to and lighting in machinery rooms.

    4.3 Installation of telephone in elevators.

    4.4 Installation of heating and ventilating equipment in the machinery room.

    4.5 Painting, other than equipment and material furnished by the Contractor.

    4.6 Furnish welding electrodes.

19. MAIN CONDENSERS.

1.0 Scope.

The Contractor shall furnish all supervision, labor, equipment, tools (under $600.00 each value) consumables, supplies, unload, store, protect, remove from storage, transport, rig, install and assemble the main condensers shells, tube sheet, internal piping and accessories and install tubes for condensers. (Figure 26)

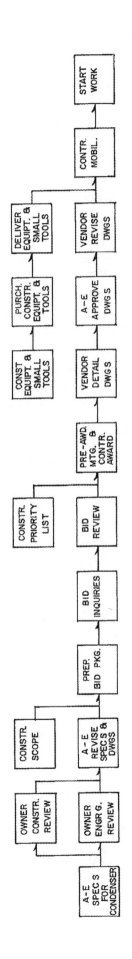

FIGURE #26

CONTRACT PACKAGE
CONDENSER ERECTION

2.0 Work By Contractor.

  2.1 The Contractor shall unload, store and protect the condenser shell, auxiliaries and condensers tubes and all other appurtenances furnished by the manufacturer. All tools furnished by the condenser manufacturer shall not be used for erection purposes but shall be stored as directed by the Construction Manager.

  2.2 The condenser erector shall unload and erect all internal and external piping, furnish with condenser, including extractor steam piping (the extraction steam and turbine drain piping) and all other piping located internal to the condensers are designated in accordance with the power piping code ANSI (USAS) 831.1.0 1967, air vapor outlet piping, and specialty items furnished with the equipment for both and main condensers and the steam generating feed pumps connections to the main condensers, such as valves, fittings and gauge glasses and other condensers trim. Furnish labor of proper jurisdiction.

  2.3 The manufacturer will shop prefit and match mark and ship in largest sections practical with nozzle attached where practical. Temporary shipping braces should not be removed unless absolutely necessary until after tube ends have been rolled. It is suggested the Bidder visit the Manufacturer's shop and inspect preassembled condenser before shipment.

  2.4 The manufacturer will furnish services to a qualified representative to oversee the erection of the condenser, installation and rolling of the tubes and testing of the complete condensers. However, this shall in no way relieve the Contractor for the entire responsibility for erection and testing of the completed condensers. The testing of the condensers and exhaust necks will be done to the entire satisfaction of the manufacturer's representative.

  2.5 The testing work shall include but not be limited to the supplying of water, filling of the condensers and dumping of the water upon completion of tests to a drainage system and thorough cleaning out of condensers after tests.

  2.6 All temporary pipe, fittings, valves, hoses, pumps, compressors, scaffolding, etc., required for each test shall be installed and removed by this Contractor.

  2.7 General cleaning of equipment and materials to be erected is this contractor's responsibility. All and only oil, grease, contaminants and other protective coatings, except shop prime coat of paint, shall be thoroughly cleaned. If any material requires cleaning as a result of Contractor's improper storage and/ or protection from the weather the cleaning shall be done by this Contractor at his expense.

  2.8 Tubes must be protected at all times from any damage; positive protection must be provided against possible tube damage from weld spatter, falling objects, chemical corrosives, etc. Openings at top of condenser must be covered and scaled against any fluid leakage from above.

  2.9 The Contractor will be required to connect equipment erected by him to the Turbine exhaust connections when released by the Turbine erector and as directed by the Construction Manager.

2.10 All welding of the condensers equipment by the Contractor shall conform to the applicable portions of current editions of the following standards and codes:
American Institute of Steel Construction-AISC
American Welding Society-AWS
American Society of Mechanical Engineers-ASME
United States Standards
831.1-February, for Pressure Piping-831.1-1967

2.11 The Contractor shall submit to the Engineer for approval certified copies and data sheets of his welding procedures and shall qualify his welders to these approved procedures as required by Section IX of the latest issue of the ASME Boiler Code.

2.12 No welding will be permitted until procedures are approved by the Engineer.

2.13 The Contractor shall properly package and surplus tubes and store as specified.

2.14 Storage of any materials will not be permitted in the building.

2.15 All survey and layout from project control points established by Owner.

2.16 Power extension from load centers, compressed air, bottles gas and air, sanitary facilities including maintenance thereof until construction sanitary facilities are in service.

3.0 Construction Procedures and QA/QC Requirements.

3.1 The Contractor shall comply with Quality Assurance requirements as delineated in the specification and referenced codes and standards.

3.2 The Contractor shall submit for approval his complete Quality Assurance Program which shall be in conformance with the Quality Assurance Criteria for Fossil Power Plants.

3.3 Contractor shall submit detailed Quality Assurance control procedures as required by the Engineer's specifications.

3.4 Contractor shall initiate construction installation procedures in detail for all work within his scope. The procedures shall include but not be limited to the following; erection or materials conformance with specifications, drawings, codes, welding procedures, certified data sheets of welding procedures, stress relieving procedures, erection sequence and shop fabrication procedures and controls, quality control checklist, calibration of test equipment and tools, alignment devices and procedures for maintenance of alignment and erection tolerances and calibration field precision instruments.

3.5 Construction procedures shall conform to applicable codes and the Engineer's specifications. All construction installation procedures shall be reviewed by the construction Managers; work shall not start until procedures have been reviewed and approved in writing. A deviation from approved procedures will require an addendum which must be approved in writing by the construction Managers prior to resuming the specific work in question.

3.6 The Contractor shall furnish materials and perform all work in accordance with specifications, drawings, including notes thereon, referenced specifications, all applicable codes and procedures, and in conformance with all local, state and federal codes and regulations. Submittals of materials and drawings shall be as specified elsewhere in the contract document.

4.0 Work Not Included.
    4.1 Installation of Turbine-Generator.
    4.2 Installation of steam generator feedwater pumps and accessories.
    4.3 Installation of equipment foundation.
    4.4 Survey control points.
    4.5 Temporary power distribution system, temporary facilities, electrical work and maintenance of temporary electrical facilities, construction sanitary6 facilities.
    4.6 Supply of all concrete.
    4.7 Furnish the condenser, tubes, piping, etc.

20. INSULATION.

1.0 Scope

The Contractor shall furnish all supervision, labor, tools (under $600.00 each value) and materials. Contractor shall unload, store, protect and/or transport and install all thermal insulation on piping and equipment as specified; in addition, the Contractor shall be fully responsible to receive and document all materials for installation by this Contractor. (Figure 27)

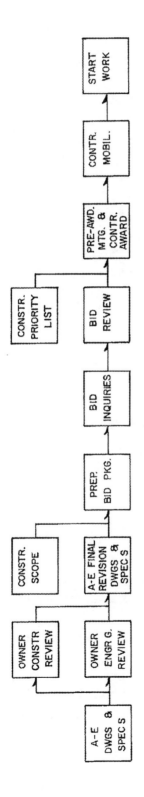

FIGURE #27

CONTRACT   PACKAGE
INSULATION

2.0 Work By Contractor.

The work shall include, but not be limited to, the following systems as applicable, including all equipment therein. Type of insulation shall include thermal, anti-sweat, personnel protective, etc. No insulation is to be applied until piping and equipment are released by Construction Managers. Insulation of equipment and pipe shall include but not be limited to the following systems:

2.1 Main Steam, Main Feedwater, Auxiliary Feedwater, Steam Generator Heat up and Circulation, Auxiliary Boiler, Diesel Generator, Diesel Fuel Oil Storage and Transfer, BOP Service Water, Nitrogen Gas, Demineralized Water Makeup, Condensate Storage, Moisture Separator Reheater Drain, H2 and CO2 Supply, Feedwater Heater Drain, Chilled Water, Primary Gas, Primary Water, Vents and Drains, Hydrogen Control, Chemical Addition and Potable Hot and Cold Water Systems where specified by Engineer.

2.2 Insulation shall include all systems and equipment.

2.3 Insulation where required for personnel protection.

2.4 Inspection stamps (ASME) and name plate on equipment shall be left exposed.

2.5 All surveying and layout from project control points established by owner.

2.6 All temporary facilities including warehouses and shops as required; power extension from load centers, compressed air, bottles gas and air, sanitary facilities including maintenance thereof, and drinking and construction water from designated onsite source.

2.7 Fireproofing of structural members, if required.

3.0 Construction Procedures and QA/QC Requirements.

3.1 The Contractor shall comply and conform to Quality Assurance requirements as delineated in the specifications and referenced codes and standards.

3.2 The Contractor shall submit for approval his complete Quality Assurance Program which shall be in conformance with the Quality Assurance Criteria for Fossil Power Plants.

3.3 Contractor shall submit detailed Quality Assurance control procedures as required by the Engineer's specification.

3.4 Contactor shall initiate construction installation procedures in detail for all work within his scope. The procedures shall include but not be limited to the following: installation of materials in conformance with specifications, drawings, codes, and Quality Control checklist and installation tolerance.

3.5 Construction procedures shall conform to applicable codes, OSHA regulations and the Engineer's specifications. All construction installation procedures shall be reviewed by the Construction Managers; work shall not start until procedures have been reviewed and approved in writing. A deviation from approved procedures will require an addendum which must be approved in writing by the Construction Managers prior to resuming the specific work in question.

3.6 The Contractor shall furnish materials and perform all work in accordance with specifications, drawings, including notes thereon, referenced specifications, all applicable codes and procedures, and in conformance wit all local, state and federal codes and regulations. Submittals of materials and drawings shall be as specified elsewhere in the contract document.

3.7 The Contractor's attention is called to the federal rules and regulations governing use of materials in his class of work specifically, Department of Labor, Occupational Safety and Health Administration (29CFR, Part 1910) and all of this Act's sub paragraphs.

3.8 The Contractor shall submit procedures and organizational supervision to be followed for and to insure compliance with new OSHA regulations to the Construction Manager for approval before any work is preformed.

4.0 Work Not Included.

4.1 Testing of all equipment and piping to be insulated.

4.2 Painting of pipe, equipment hangers, etc.

4.3 Insulation of HVAC ductwork and equipment, T-G equipment and boiler.

4.4 Insulation work on systems as specified in contract by Engineer.

21. STRUCTURAL STEEL

1.0 Scope

The Contractor shall provide all supervision, labor, services, new materials, tools and equipment to detail, fabricate, furnish, shop prime coat, deliver, unload, store, protect, transport and erect the structural steel required for Diesel Generator Building, Control Building, Service Buildings as specified. (Figure 28)

Robert E. Bartz

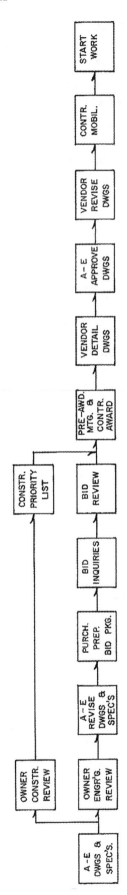

FIGURE #28

CONTRACT PACKAGE
STRUCTURAL STEEL

2.0 Work By Contractor.

    2.1 Detail, furnish, fabricate and erect structural steel, steel metal decking except metal deck for roof slabs, crane rails and monorails attached to structural for the building structures as specified as follows:

        2.1.1 Control Building

        2.1.2 Service and Circulating Water Pump House Building.

        2.1.3 Administration and Service Building.

        2.1.4 Diesel Generator Building.

    2.2 Furnish and install all stairways (stringer and treads) and handrail attached to structural, miscellaneous steel, stairway, hand railing, floor plate, grating, etc., as noted on drawings and where specified.

    2.3 Provide continuous inspection and reports of high strength bolting during structural steel erection period including calibration of torque wrenches and torque testing of all bolted connections.

    2.4 Shop prime steel with paint and color as specified.

    2.5 All surveying and layout from project control points established by Owner.

    2.6 All temporary facilities including field offices, changehouses, warehouses and shops as required, power extensions from load centers, compressed air, bottled gas and air, sanitary facilities including maintenance thereof and drinking and construction water from designated onsite source.

    2.7 Clean up areas associate with Contractor's scope of work.

3.0 Construction Procedures and QA/QC Requirements.

    3.1 Contractor shall comply and conform to Quality Assurance requirements as delineated in the specifications and referenced codes and standards.

    3.2 The Contractor shall submit for approval his complete Quality Assurance Program which shall be in conformance with the Quality Assurance Criteria for Fossil Fuel Power Plants.

    3.3 The Contractor shall submit detailed Quality Assurance and Quality Control procedures as required by Engineer's specifications.

    3.4 The Contractor shall submit for approval detailed written construction and inspection procedures as applicable to the contract scope of work.

    3.5 The above data and detailed written construction procedures must be submitted to the Engineer for approval before starting any phase of work within scope of this contract.

4.0 Work Not Included.

    4.1 Structural concrete.

    4.2 Anchor bolts and steel embedded in concrete.

    4.3 Miscellaneous steel, floor plate, grating and stairways and handrail not attached to structural steel, unless otherwise noted on the drawings.

    4.4 Field touch-up and finish coating painting.

    4.5 Grouting of structural steel column base plates.

    4.6 Furnish and install metal roof decking.

4.7 Detail, furnish and erect structural steel for boiler and turbine areas.

4.8 Furnish welding electrodes.

22. FIELD FABRICATED TANKS

1.0 Scope

The Contractor shall furnish all supervision, labor, tools, new materials and equipment to design, detail, fabricate, deliver, unload, store and/or transport, erect, finish primer coat of exterior surfaces of carbon steel tanks and touch-up weld joints, etc., and test all field fabricated tanks. (Figure 29)

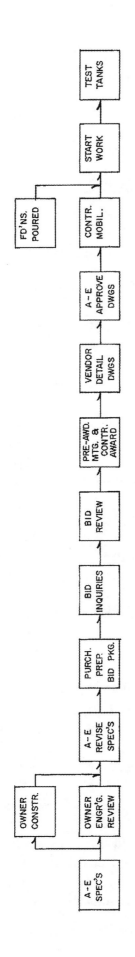

FIGURE #29

CONTRACT PACKAGE
FIELD FABRICATED
TANKS

2.0 Work By Contractor.

The work shall include but not be limited to the following:

2.1 Fuel Oil Metering tanks.

2.2 Fuel Oil Storage tanks.

2.3 Condensate Storage tanks.

2.4 Diesel tanks.

2.5 Testing of tanks as required by the specifications.

2.6 Furnish all NDT test procedures and documentation.

2.7 Furnish all welding procedures and perform welder qualification tests per applicable codes and specifications.

2.8 Finishing all welds to specified tolerances.

2.9 All hydrostatic tests of tanks shall be performed by use of demineralized water.

2.10 Contractor shall furnish all piping and valves and connections to and from equipment to be tested and furnish equipment, piping and valves to dispose of water from tested components.

2.11 All surveying and layout from project survey control points established by Owner.

2.12 All temporary facilities including offices, changehoused, warehouses and shops as required, power extension from load centers, compressed, bottled gas and air, sanitary facilities including maintenance thereof until construction facilities are available and drinking and construction water from designated on site source.

3.0 Construction Procedures and QA/QC Requirements.

3.1 The Contractor shall comply and conform to Quality Assurance requirements as delineated in the specifications and referenced codes and standards.

3.2 The Contractor shall submit for approval his complete Quality Assurance Program which shall be in conformance with Quality Assurance Criteria for Fossil Fuel Power Plants.

3.3 Contractor shall submit detailed Quality Assurance control procedures as required by the Engineer's specification.

3.4 Contractor shall initiate construction installation procedures in detail for all work within his scope. The procedures shall include but not be limited to the following: erection of materials for liner in conformance with specifications, drawings, codes, welding procedures, certified data sheets of welding procedures, stress relieving procedures, erection sequence and shop fabrication procedures and controls, quality control checklist, calibration of test equipment and tools, alignment and erection tolerances and calibration field precision instruments.

3.5 Construction procedures shall conform to applicable codes and the Engineer's specifications. All construction installation procedures shall be reviewed by the Construction Managers; work shall not start until procedures have been reviewed and approved in writing. A deviation from approved procedures will require an addendum which must be approved in writing by the Construction Managers prior to resuming the specific work in question.

3.6 The contractor shall furnish materials and perform all work in accordance with specifications; drawings, including notes therein, referenced specifications: all applicable codes and procedures, and in conformance with all local, state and federal codes and regulations. Submittals of materials and drawings shall be as specified elsewhere in the contract documents.

4.0 Work Not Included.

4.1 Concrete foundations and structures.

4.2 Embedded anchors or anchor bolts (except those attached to Contractor's work), unless otherwise specified.

4.3 Structural steel supports except as noted.

4.4 Insulation.

4.5 Furnishing demineral water for test purposes.

4.6 Survey control points.

4.7 Furnish welding electrodes.

23. ARCHITECTURAL TREATMENT.

1.0 Scope

The Contractor shall provide all supervision, labor, services, new materials, tools(under $600.00 each value) and equipment to detail, fabricate, furnish, shop prime coat materials where specified, deliver, unload, store, protect, transport and install sash, doors, ceilings, floor finishes, glass and glazing as required for the Control Building, Turbine Building, Service and Circulating Water Pump House and Administration and Service Buildings, EFC as indicated on the drawings and specified by the Engineer. (Figure 30)

FIGURE #30

CONTRACT PACKAGE
ARCHITECTURAL TREATMENT
& MASONRY

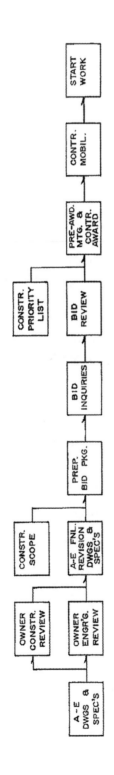

2.0 Work By Contractor
    2.1 The Engineer will provide performance type specifications as a guide to the Contractor to procure materials also for installation for the scope of the work. These specifications shall include but not be limited to the following:
        2.1.1   Sash-all types including weather strippings.
        2.1.2   Doors-all types (hollow metal and frame-UL type).
        2.1.3   Doors-motor operated and manually operated rolling doors and operators.
        2.1.4   Ceilings-acoustical, standard gypsum board fascias, lath and plaster.
        2.1.5   Glass and glazing-all strengths, translucent panels, control room windows.
        2.1.6   Floor finishes-quarry tile, ceramic mosaic tile, resilient tile and sheet flooring, special surface treatments.
        2.1.7   Hardware, complete hardware schedule for all architectural treatment.
        2.1.8   Metal or fabricated partitions and panels.

    2.2 The Contractor shall submit samples when practical of materials to be furnished for engineer's approval.
    2.3 All necessary caulking shall be included where specified.
    2.4 Contractor shall provide Engineer with required copies of all operating and maintenance manuals for materials specified.
    2.5 The Contractor shall install all work in accordance with building codes and standards, applicable in the state.
    2.6 The Contractor shall survey and layout all work from established control points by Owner.
    2.7 The Contractor shall furnish and install temporary facilities including changehouse, warehouse and shops as required: power extensions from designated load centers, compressed air, bottled gas and all heating and temporary heating for protection of work within the scope of this contract, drinking water and construction water from a designated source.

3.0 Construction Procedures and QA/QC Requirements.
    3.1 The Contractor shall comply and conform to Quality Assurance requirements as delineated in the specifications and referenced coded and standards.
    3.2 The Contractor shall submit for approval his complete Quality Assurance Program which shall be in conformance with the Quality Assurance Criteria for Fossil Power Plants.
    3.3 Contractor shall submit detailed Quality Assurance control procedures as required by the Engineer's specification.
    3.4 Contractor shall initiate construction installation procedures in detail for all work within his scope. The procedures shall include but be limited to the following: erection of materials in conformance with specifications, drawings, codes, erection sequence and shop fabrication procedures and controls, Quality Control checklist and erection tolerances.

3.5 Construction procedures shall conform to applicable codes and the Engineer's specifications. All construction installation procedures shall be reviewed by the Construction Managers; work shall not start until procedures have been reviewed and approved in writing. A deviation from approved procedures will require an addendum which must be approved in writing by the Construction Manager prior to resuming the specific work in question.

3.6 The Contractor shall furnish materials and perform all work in accordance with specifications; drawings, including notes thereon; referenced specifications, all applicable codes and procedures; and in conformance with all local, state and federal codes and regulations. Submittals of materials and drawings shall be as specified elsewhere in the contract documents.

4.0 Work Not Included.

4.1 Installation of project temporary power distribution system, temporary electrical work, maintenance of temporary electrical system for project.

4.2 Survey control points.

4.3 Concrete work.

4.4 Furnish and erect metal siding.

4.5 Furnish and install masonry.

4.6 Leaded glass windows for drum handling area in Waste Process Building.

4.7 Finished painting.

4.8 Furnish welding electrode.

MASONRY

1.0 Scope

1.1 The Contractor shall furnish and install all masonry including block, brick reinforcing, lintels, embedments as shown on drawings and as described in the Engineer's specification.

1.2 All concrete masonry units shall be heavy weight type and shall be solid load-bearing, or hollow not-load-bearing as specified.

2.0 Work By Contractor.

2.1 The Contractor shall furnish and install all masonry materials as specified in accordance with the latest revisions to referenced codes and standards.

2.2 The Contractor shall place embedments as work progresses and lintels, loose structural steel; miscellaneous metal items, inserts, sleeves, anchors, flashing and similar miscellaneous items shall be built in as work progresses, but installed by others.

2.3 All masonry shall be laid plumb and true to line with level courses and accurately spaced with a story pole and bonding shall be as specified.

2.4 Joints shall be nominally 3/8 inch, except where other joint thickness is specified.

2.5 The Contractor shall provide for sealing and caulking of joints on the weather side as specified.

2.6 The Contractor shall provide protection during construction of all surfaces of masonry not being worked on, and during inclement weather tops of exposed masonry walls shall be covered with strong, waterproof membrane and well secured in place.

2.7 Contractor shall provide all temporary heat and enclosures to protect his work from freezing. Masonry work of any kind shall not be laid when temperature is below 40 degrees F or likely to fall below 40 degrees F within 24 hours, except and unless written permission is granted, all materials shall be heated and a suitable heated enclosure shall be provided; methods of heating and enclosure shall be approved by Construction Manager.

2.8 The Contractor shall protect the masonry from freezing for 48 hours after it has been laid.

2.9 The Contractor shall be responsible to provide adequate provisions during construction to protect masonry against wind damage.

2.10 The Contractor shall submit samples of all masonry materials to Engineer for approval and he shall provide manufacturer's certificates which certify that all materials which the manufacturer supplies meet all the requirements of Engineer's codes and standards as specified.

2.11 The Contractor shall erect sample panels of masonry work to be installed in the project. The sample panel walls shall be 5'0 long by 4'0 high and they shall be erected where specified by the Construction Manager. Upon approval by the Engineer, the erection of permanent masonry construction shall proceed.

2.12 Contractor shall provide for all surveying and layout of his work from project control points established by the Owner.

2.13 The Contractor shall provide all temporary facilities including offices, warehouses and hops as required; power extension from load centers; compressed air; bottles gas and air; and drinking and construction water from designated onsite source.

3.0 Construction Procedures and QA/QC Requirements.

3.1 The Contractor shall comply and conform to Quality Assurance requirements as delineated in the specifications and referenced codes and standards.

3.2 The Contractor shall submit for approval his complete Quality Assurance Program which shall be in conformance with the Quality Assurance Criteria for Fossil Power Plants.

3.3 Contractor shall submit detailed Quality Assurance control procedures as required by the Engineer's specification.

3.4 Contractor shall initiate construction installation procedures in detail for all work within his scope. The procedures shall include but not be limited to the following: erection of materials in conformance with specifications, drawings, codes and Quality control checklist.

3.5 Construction procedures shall conform to applicable codes and the Engineer's specifications. All construction installation procedures shall be reviewed by the Construction Managers; work shall not start until procedures have been reviewed and approved in writing by the Construction Managers prior to resuming the specific work in question.

3.6 The Contractor shall furnish materials and perform all work in accordance with specifications; drawings, including notes thereon; referenced specifications; all applicable codes and procedures; and in conformance with all local, state and federal codes and regulations. Submittals of materials and drawings shall be as specified elsewhere in the contract documents.

3.7 No additional tests beyond those normally employed either in manufacturing, installation or construction processes or as called for by the specified codes and standards are required for the masonry contract.

3.8 The Contractor's attention is called to the federal rules and regulations governing use of materials in the class of work specifically, Department of Labor, Occupational Safety and Health Administration (29CFR, Part 1910), and all of this Act's subparagraphs.

4.0 Work Not Included.

4.1 Architectural treatments, including metal door bucks, windows, sash, hardware, etc.

4.2 Finished painting.

4.3 Inserts in elevator shaft enclosures, etc.

4.4 Survey control points.

4.5 Fabricated reinforcing steel.

4.6 Concrete delivery or placement.

4.7 Structural steel and attachments.

4.8 Temporary power distribution system, temporary electrical work, and maintenance of temporary electrical facilities.

24. PAINTING AND SPECIAL COATINGS

1.0 Scope

1.1 Contractor shall furnish all equipment and materials necessary for all surface preparation; furnishing paint, tools and materials for all buildings, structures and equipment as specified and listed in Engineer's painting schedule. (Figure 31)

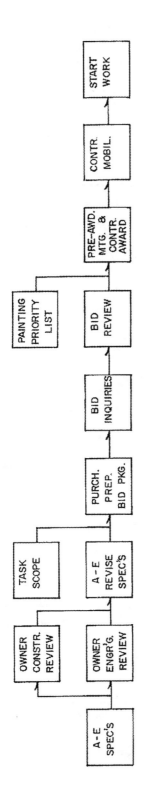

FIGURE #31

CONTRACT PACKAGE
PAINTING

2.0 Work By Contractor.

2.1 Contractor shall furnish pigment paint in containers not larger than five gallon containers and paint shall be delivered in quantities sufficiently in advance of need to avoid delays and/or interruptions in work due to lack of materials. Paint shall be in unbroken containers that show at time of use the designated color, date of manufacturers, formula or specification number and manufacturer's direction for use and name of manufacturer.

2.2 Protection by drop cloths of the work of other trades and the spattering of paint on finished equipment is the responsibility of this Contractor and shall be avoided.

2.3 All surfaces to be painted must be thoroughly clean of accumulation of dirt, grease, oil and any contaminant by washing with detergent and water. Loose material may be blown off with air and/or use of vacuum cleaners and stiff bristle brushes.

2.4 The Contractor shall paint all items listed in Engineer's painting schedule including structural steel, all ferrous pipes not insulated, pipe hangers, valves, electric conduits, fabric covered insulate pipe and equipment following Engineer's specified instructions.

2.5 Before painting and engineered safety pipe systems, conduit and equipment, Contractor must consult with Engineer and/or Construction Manager for color coding identification and instructions.

2.6 All materials and surfaces which have not been previously primed shall be primed as specified before applying finish coats. Protective coats (by vendor) shall be removed where specified by Engineer.

2.7 Contractor shall promptly submit two samples of all paint colors on suitable metal panels (6"x9") to Engineer for approval. No painting shall be applied unless approved by Engineer.

2.8 Provide template and paint identification codes, numbers, signs, etc.

2.9 Touch up paint where required.

2.10 Maintain inventory record of all paints and coatings to preclude use of material beyond recommended "shelf life".

2.11 Painting of concealed surfaces.

2.12 Provide paint storage facilities outside the permanent building area which are safe, fireproof, well ventilated, etc.

2.13 All temporary facilities including offices, changehouses, warehouses and shops as required; power extension from load centers; compressed air; bottled gas and air; sanitary facilities including maintenance thereof until construction sanitary facilities are in service; and drinking and construction water from designated onsite source.

2.14 Contractor shall provide paint performance tests performed by an independent laboratory for all specified paint mixtures.

2.15 Contractor shall furnish all equipment and materials necessary to maintain humidity and temperatures as specified by Engineer and/or paint supplier.

2.16 Contractor shall initiate construction installation procedures in detail for all work within his scope. Contractor shall be responsible for the preparation of written procedures describing how the work under these specifications will be carried out. These shall include methods of:

2.16.1 Light sandblasting.

2.16.2 Acid etching.

2.16.3 Application and curing.

2.16.4 Inspection methods.

2.17 Contractor shall set forth how surface preparation will be checked, how thickness of coating is obtained, the curing of items for coating, etc. The procedures shall include as a minimum the following sections, which shall be Quality control checked to ensure that:

2.17.1 The surface is properly prepared.

2.17.2 The coatings are properly mixed.

2.17.3 The coatings are applied properly (manufacturer's recommendations are applicable to the above).

2.17.4 No runs, sags or pinholes are present in coatings.

2.17.5 The wet film thickness is correct.

2.17.6 Each coat is cured properly prior to applying the next coat.

2.17.7 The final coat is smooth and free from sharp protrusions, pockets and pinholes.

2.17.8 The dry film thickness is determined with a nondestructive dry film thickness gauge.

2.17.9 Additional coats over areas showing pinholes and holidays are applied properly.

2.18 Documentation of the above inspection shall be furnished by Contractor on a timely basis as work progresses.

2.19 The Contractor shall furnish materials and perform all work in accordance with specifications; drawings, including notes thereon; referenced specifications; all applicable codes and procedures; and in conformance with all local, state and federal codes and regulations. Submittals of materials and drawings shall be as specified elsewhere in the contract documents.

3.0 Construction Procedures and QA/QC Requirements. (For Phases I, II, and III).

3.1 The contractor shall comply and conform to Quality Assurance requirements as delineated in the specifications and referenced codes and standards.

3.2 The Contractor shall submit for approval his complete Quality Assurance Program which shall be in conformance with the United States Atomic Energy Commission Rules and Regulations, 10CFR-50-Licensing of Production and Utilization Facilities, Appendix B.

4.0 Work Not Included.

4.1 Substation and transmission towers.

4.2 Factory finished mechanical and electrical items unless otherwise specified.

4.3 Galvanized grating and treads.

    4.4 Non-ferrous metals.

    4.5 Aluminum jacketed insulations.

    4.6 Pipe to be insulated.

25. SIDING.

1.0 Scope

The Contractor shall provide all supervision, labor, tools (under $600.00 each value) and new material to furnish and install the protected metal siding; and miscellaneous flashing materials as require by the specifications and drawings. (Figure 32)

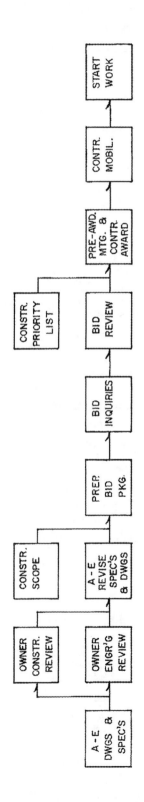

FIGURE #32

**CONTRACT PACKAGE
SIDING**

2.0 The work shall include but not be limited to the following:

    2.1 Furnish and install protected metal siding and external louvers, and perform all cutouts and metal flashing of cutouts and openings as required.

    2.2 Surveying and layout from project survey control points established by the Owner.

    2.3 All temporary facilities including offices, changehouses, warehouses and ships as required; power extension from load centers; compressed air; bottled gas; sanitary facilities including maintenance thereof until drinking and construction water from designated onsite source.

3.0 Work Not Included.

    3.1 Structural, mechanical and electrical work except as specified and specifically shown on the drawings.

    3.2 Finish painting.

    3.3 Project survey control points.

    3.4 Metal floor decking.

ROOFING AND FLASHING

1.1 Scope

The contractor shall provide all supervision, labor, tools, new materials and equipment to furnish and install metal roof deck, built up roofing and miscellaneous flashing materials as required for all buildings by the specifications and drawings

1.2 Work By Contractor.

    2.1 Install metal roof deck and perform all cutouts and openings as required; furnish and install all metal flashing and counter flashings; furnish and install all built up roofing as specified and pre cast concrete walkways planks if required.

    2.2 Surveying and layout from project control points established by Owner.

    2.3 All temporary facilities including offices, changehouses, warehouses and shops as required; power extension from load centers; compressed air; bottled gas; and drinking and construction water from designated onsite source.

1.3 Work Not Included.

    3.1 Structural, mechanical and electrical work.

    3.2 Finish painting.

    3.3 Project survey control points.

    3.4 Metal floor decking.

    3.5 Furnish welding electrodes.

26 FINAL ROAD WORK.

1.0 Scope

1.1 The Contractor shall furnish all materials and supervision, labor, services, new materials, tools and equipment to install all paving, curbs, culverts and drainage ditches as shown on Engineer's drawing and as specified.

1.2 The work shall include cutting, filling and preparation of sub grade, fine grading to lay base course and install asphalt paving as specified for plant roads and parking areas.

1.3 All ditching and culverts are included and they shall drain as shown on drawings or as specified by Engineer. (Figure 33)

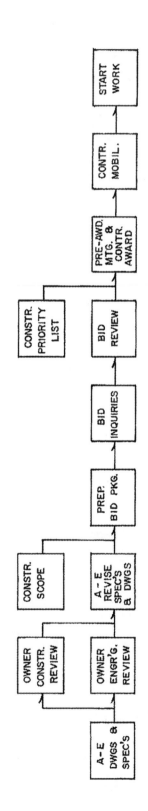

FIGURE #33

CONTRACT PACKAGE
FINAL ROAD WORK
& GRADING

2.0 Work By Contractor.

    2.1 The contractor shall install all wok for all plant roads and parking areas as shown on drawing and as specified by Engineer, and in accordance with the current codes of the state Public works and Highways, American Association of State Highway Official Standards and other referenced standards.

    2.2 Inspection of all work will be preformed by Construction Managers as the work progresses. Faulty work and work not conforming to Engineer's specification and the drawings shall be removed and repaired at the Contractor's expense.

    2.3 The Contractor shall perform the work in a sequence and in a time schedule satisfactory to and approved by Construction Managers. All of the work covered by this specification shall be coordinated with the work of others. All phases of construction shall be performed in such a manner as not to interfere with the normal operation of the plant.

    2.4 The Contractor shall examine the areas on which, and against which, his work is to be applied. It shall be his responsibility to notify the Construction Managers in writing of any defects in the area of his work, which in his opinion, would be detrimental to the installation or quality of his work. The Contractor shall not commence operations until all such conditions are remedied to the satisfaction of himself and the Construction Managers. Once the Contractor has commenced the installation of the road work, he shall assume full responsibility for the acceptability of all areas where the roads are to be installed. The Contractor shall be responsible for the protection of these areas until the completion of his work.

    2.5 It shall be the Contractor's responsibility to ensure that all buildings, surfaces and equipment in the vicinity of his work shall be adequately protected against damage during the fulfillment of this contract.

    2.6 At completion, the Contractor shall clean and repair any work which has been marred or damaged in the course of his work and leave the premises in good condition, acceptable to the Construction Managers.

    2.7 All materials, equipment and the methods of construction shall conform to the Engineer's specification and the state Public Works and Highway Department.

    2.8 Placing and compaction: The asphaltic mixture shall be laid only upon a dry, prepared base cleaned of all loose or foreign materials. Unless permitted by the Construction Manager, the asphaltic mixture shall be speared by means of a mechanical self power paver, capable of spreading the mixture true to line, grade and crown shown on the drawings. After the mixture has been screed, the surface shall be rolled with power drive rollers weighting not less than 10 tons. If only one roller is used, it shall be a tandem roller.

    2.9 All temporary facilities including field offices, changhouses are required; power extension from load centers; compressed air; bottled gas; drinking and construction water from designated onsite source.

    2.10 Clean up areas of work associated with Contractor's scope of work.

2.11 All surveying and layout from project survey control points established by Owner.

3.0 Work Not Included.
    3.1 Concrete work.
    3.2 Project survey control points.
    3.3 Temporary power distribution system, temporary facilities, electrical work and maintenance of temporary facilities, construction sanitary facilities.

FINAL SITE WORK

1.1 Scope.

The Contractor shall furnish all materials, supervision, labor, services, new materials, tools and equipment to furnish and install road signs, guard rails, barricades, sidewalks; to finish grade and landscape areas as shown on Engineer's drawings and as specified by Engineer. (Figure 33)

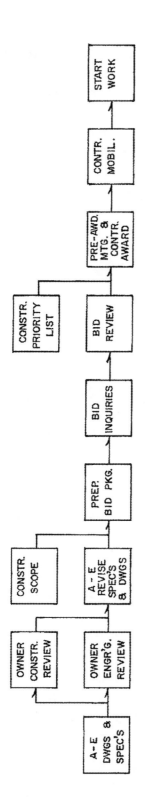

FIGURE #33

CONTRACT PACKAGE
FINAL ROAD WORK
& GRADING

1.2 Work By Contractor.

    2.1 The Contractor shall install all foundations and supports required for specified road signs and erect all signs as shown and specified by Engineer, and in accordance with current codes of state Public Works and Highways, American Association of State Highway Officials and other referenced standards.

    2.2 The Contractor shall furnish and install class of concrete sidewalks, including expansion joints, surface finished and color as shown on drawings and specified by Engineer.

    2.3 Landscaping shall be supervised by an experienced nurseryman in the employ of the Contractor.

    2.4 All finished grading and landscaping shall conform to Landscape Architect's drawings and specifications including but not limited to selective thinning of trees in designated areas, top soiling,

27. FENCING.

1.0 Scope

The Contractor shall provide supervision, labor, tools, materials and equipment to furnish and install the temporary and permanent fencing and gates as shown on the drawings. (Figure 34)

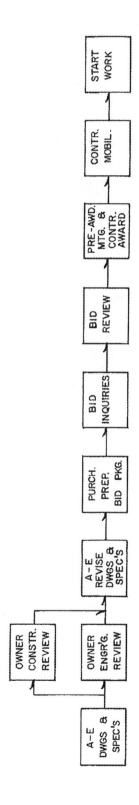

FIGURE #34

CONTRACT PACKAGE
PERMANENT FENCE

1.2 Work By Contractor.

The work shall include but not be limited to the following:

2.1 Excavate for fence and gate posts.

2.2 Furnish, install, plumb and align fence and gate posts and encase in concrete as specified.

2.3 Furnish and install wire fabric and barbed wire as specified.

2.4 Furnish and install gates as shown on the drawings.

2.5 Dismantle, relocate or dispose of temporary fencing and gates as specified.

2.6 Backfill post holes.

2.7 All surveying and layout from project survey control points established by Owner.

2.8 All temporary facilities including office, changehouse and shop as required; power extension from load centers; sanitary facilities until permanent facilities are available; and drinking and construction water from designated onsite source.

1.3 Work Not Included.

3.1 General Grading.

3.2 Furnish concrete and rebar.

3.3 Electrical work if required.

3.4 Sanitary facilities.

3.5 Project survey control points.

CHAPTER 5

CONTRACT SELECTION

Compatibility

When the term "contract" is used it truly is defined as an agreement for specific services. This document will have terms and conditions, A/E drawings and a construction schedule with a start up date and a finish date. The contract describes in detail the scope of the work and how it is to progress. In turn, the owner is bound to pay the contractor based on the above provisions. The contractor and owner will sign the formal contract. This means the contractor has been hired by law to provide services in accordance with the contract documents. The owner will compensate the contractor for those services provided.

The previous chapters explain the manner and method for selecting the most economical and beneficial contract that will meet the owner's needs, using customer flow chart. (Figure 35)

CUSTOMER FLOW CHART

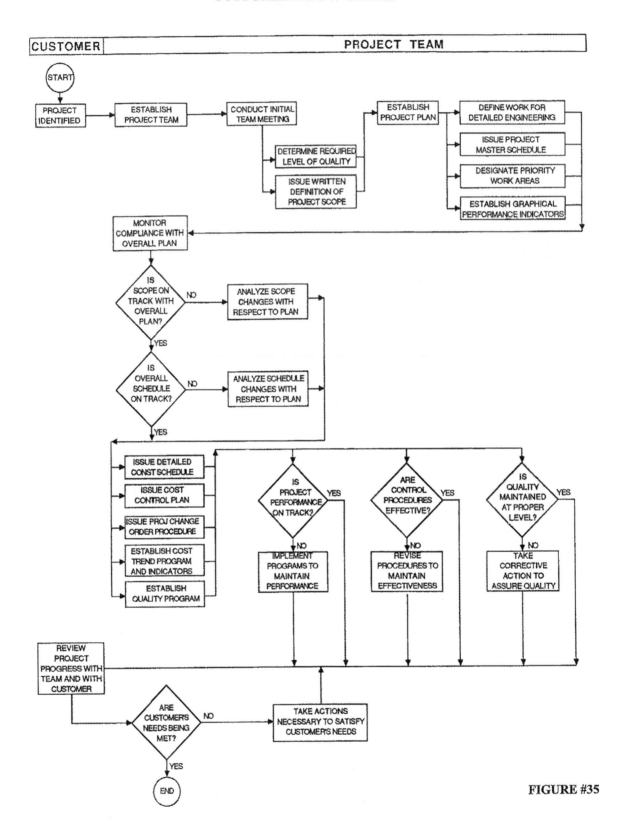

FIGURE #35

Selection of a Contract

There are eighteen (18) basic types of contracts that are most frequently used. They are:

Lump Sum (Figure 36)
Unit Price (Figure 37)
Cost-Plus Percentage (Figure 38)
Cost Plus Fixed Price (Figure 39)
Single Contract (Figure 40)
Construction Management (Figure 41)
Design/Build Lump Sum (Figure 42)
Phased Packages (Figure 43)
Lease Purchase Option I-Standard (Figure 44)
Lease Purchase Option II-Phased Packages (Figure 45)
Lease Purchase Option III-Design/Build (Figure 46)
Construction Management/Lump Sum (Figure 47)
Construction Management/Contract Packages (Figure 48)
Project Management (Figure 49)
Multiple Packages/Trades (Figure 50)
Turnkey-Lump Sum (Figure 51)
Fast Track (Figure 52)
Construction Management w/Contract Packages and Force Account (Figure 53)

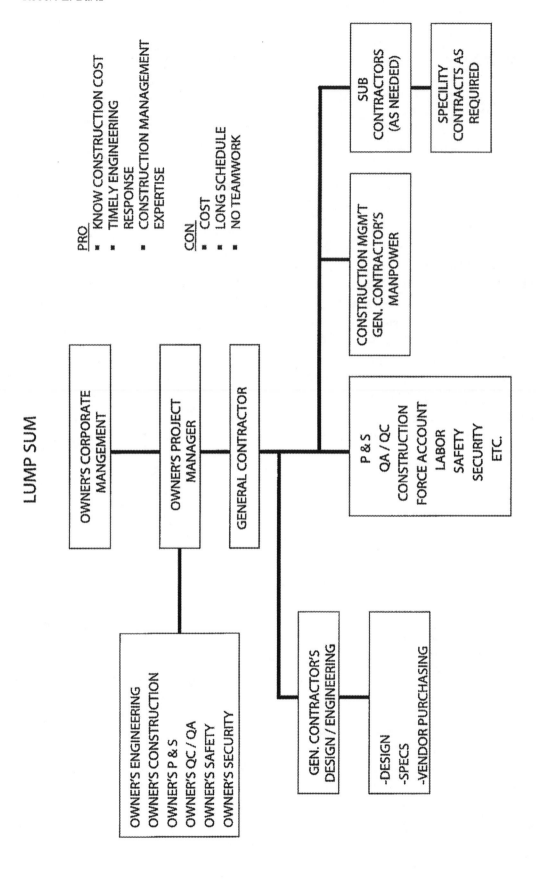

LUMP SUM

PRO
- KNOW CONSTRUCTION COST
- TIMELY ENGINEERING RESPONSE
- CONSTRUCTION MANAGEMENT EXPERTISE

CON
- COST
- LONG SCHEDULE
- NO TEAMWORK

OWNER'S CORPORATE MANGEMENT

OWNER'S PROJECT MANAGER

GENERAL CONTRACTOR

OWNER'S ENGINEERING
OWNER'S CONSTRUCTION
OWNER'S P & S
OWNER'S QC / QA
OWNER'S SAFETY
OWNER'S SECURITY

GEN. CONTRACTOR'S DESIGN / ENGINEERING

-DESIGN
-SPECS
-VENDOR PURCHASING

P & S
QA / QC
CONSTRUCTION
FORCE ACCOUNT
LABOR
SAFETY
SECURITY
ETC.

CONSTRUCTION MGM'T GEN. CONTRACTOR'S MANPOWER

SUB CONTRACTORS (AS NEEDED)

SPECILTY CONTRACTS AS REQUIRED

FIGURE #36

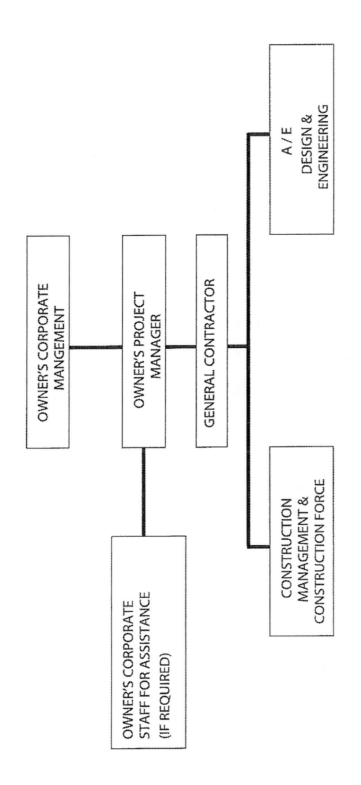

UNIT PRICE CONTRACT

OWNER'S CORPORATE MANGEMENT

OWNER'S PROJECT MANAGER

GENERAL CONTRACTOR

A / E DESIGN & ENGINEERING

OWNER'S CORPORATE STAFF FOR ASSISTANCE (IF REQUIRED)

CONSTRUCTION MANAGEMENT & CONSTRUCTION FORCE

KEY ISSUES
1. BASED ON ESTIMATED QUANTITIES
2. CONTRACTOR PAID FOR SUM ACTUALLY REMOVE
3. PAID EXTRA IF MORE THAN ESTIMATED
4. DISAGREEMENT IN REMOVED MATERIAL
5. P&S NOT ABLE TO KEEP UP
6. QUALITY WORKMANSHIP
7. SUFFICIENT MANPOWER & EQUIPMENT

FIGURE #37

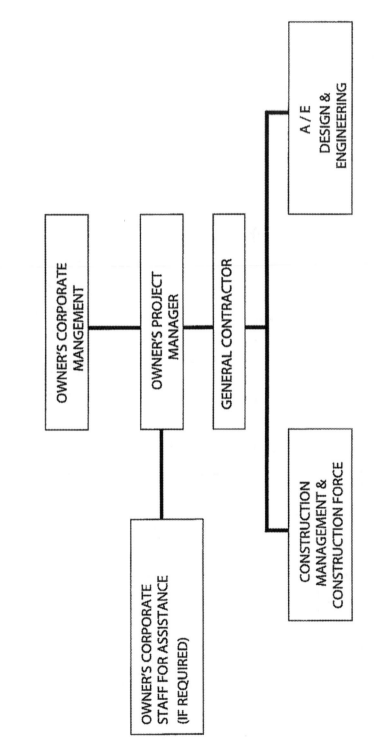

COST PLUS PERCENTAGE CONTRACT

OWNER'S CORPORATE MANGEMENT

OWNER'S PROJECT MANAGER

GENERAL CONTRACTOR

OWNER'S CORPORATE STAFF FOR ASSISTANCE (IF REQUIRED)

A / E DESIGN & ENGINEERING

CONSTRUCTION MANAGEMENT & CONSTRUCTION FORCE

KEY ISSUES
1. POOR STATUS OF ENGINEERING
2. DETERMINING CONTRACTOR'S FEE IS IN NEGOTIATED CONTRACT. PERCENT OF COST IS NOT KNOWN
3. NO ADVANCEMENT OF A/E DATE

FIGURE #38

142

FIGURE #39

COST PLUS FIX PRICE CONTRACT

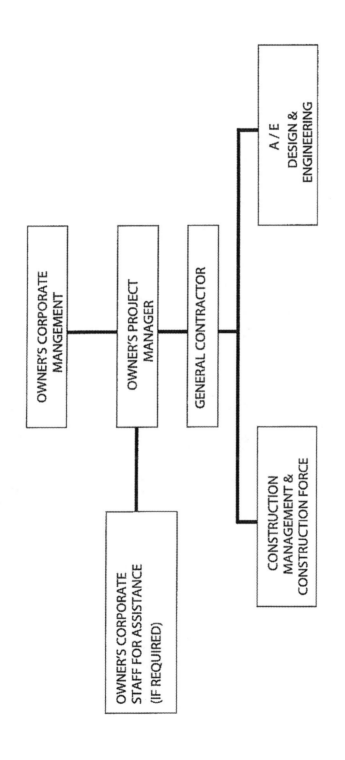

OWNER'S CORPORATE MANGEMENT

OWNER'S PROJECT MANAGER

OWNER'S CORPORATE STAFF FOR ASSISTANCE (IF REQUIRED)

GENERAL CONTRACTOR

A / E DESIGN & ENGINEERING

CONSTRUCTION MANAGEMENT & CONSTRUCTION FORCE

KEY ISSUES
1. CONTRACTOR'S FEE IS ESTABLISHED AS A FIXED SUM
2. WORK NEEDS TO   BE WELL DEFINED
3. TIME OF CONSTRUCTION DEPENDS ON COMPLEXITY OF WORK
4. EQUIPMENT / MANPOWER UNSTABLE
5. ESTIMATE OF COST IS ONLY APPROXIMATE

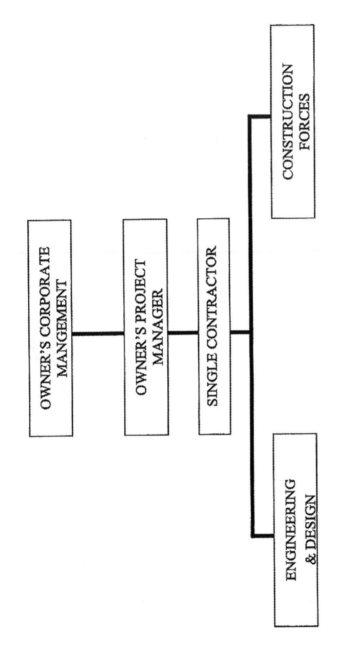

SINGLE CONTRACT

OWNER'S CORPORATE MANGEMENT

OWNER'S PROJECT MANAGER

SINGLE CONTRACTOR

CONSTRUCTION FORCES

ENGINEERING & DESIGN

PRO
- SINGLE SOURCE

CON
- POOR COMMUNICATION
- TIGHT SCHEDULES
- MANPOWER
- EQUIPMENT
- VENDORS
- OWNER FINANCED

FIGURE #40

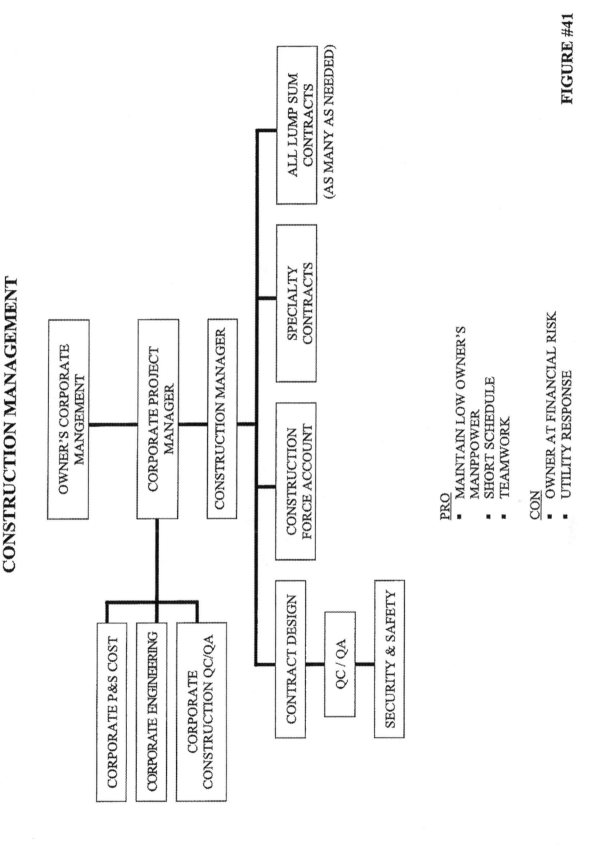

CONSTRUCTION MANAGEMENT

OWNER'S CORPORATE MANGEMENT

CORPORATE PROJECT MANAGER

CONSTRUCTION MANAGER

CORPORATE P&S COST

CORPORATE ENGINEERING

CORPORATE CONSTRUCTION QC/QA

CONSTRUCTION FORCE ACCOUNT

SPECIALTY CONTRACTS

ALL LUMP SUM CONTRACTS
(AS MANY AS NEEDED)

CONTRACT DESIGN

QC / QA

SECURITY & SAFETY

PRO
* MAINTAIN LOW OWNER'S MANPPOWER
* SHORT SCHEDULE
* TEAMWORK

CON
* OWNER AT FINANCIAL RISK
* UTILITY RESPONSE

FIGURE #41

145

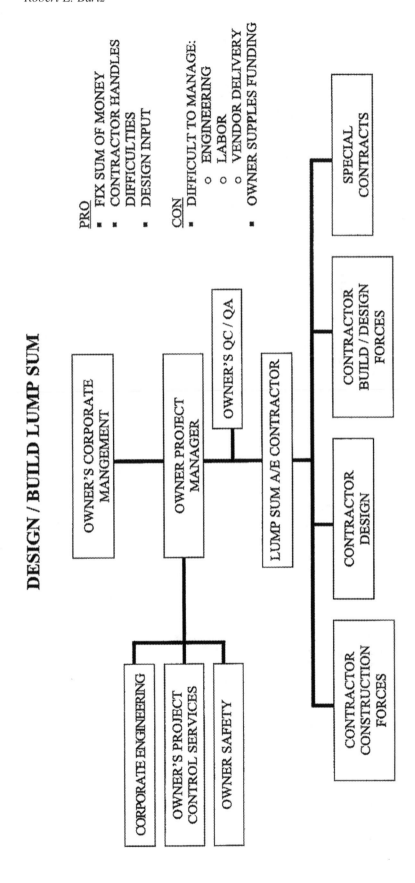

Robert E. Bartz

DESIGN / BUILD LUMP SUM

PRO
- FIX SUM OF MONEY
- CONTRACTOR HANDLES DIFFICULTIES
- DESIGN INPUT

CON
- DIFFICULT TO MANAGE:
  - ENGINEERING
  - LABOR
  - VENDOR DELIVERY
- OWNER SUPPLES FUNDING

OWNER'S CORPORATE MANGEMENT

OWNER PROJECT MANAGER

OWNER'S QC / QA

LUMP SUM A/E CONTRACTOR

CORPORATE ENGINEERING

OWNER'S PROJECT CONTROL SERVICES

OWNER SAFETY

CONTRACTOR DESIGN

CONTRACTOR BUILD / DESIGN FORCES

SPECIAL CONTRACTS

CONTRACTOR CONSTRUCTION FORCES

FIGURE #42

146

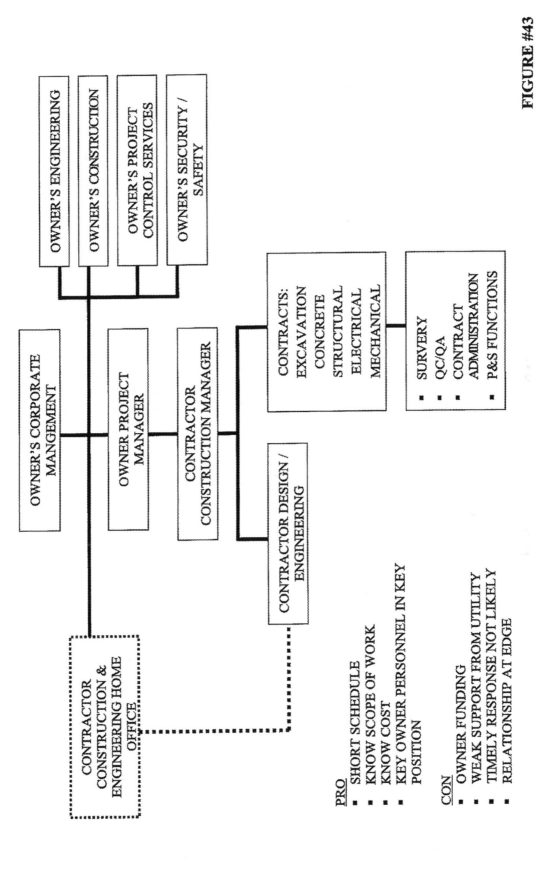

PHASED (MINIMUM) PACKAGES

FIGURE #43

147

Robert E. Bartz

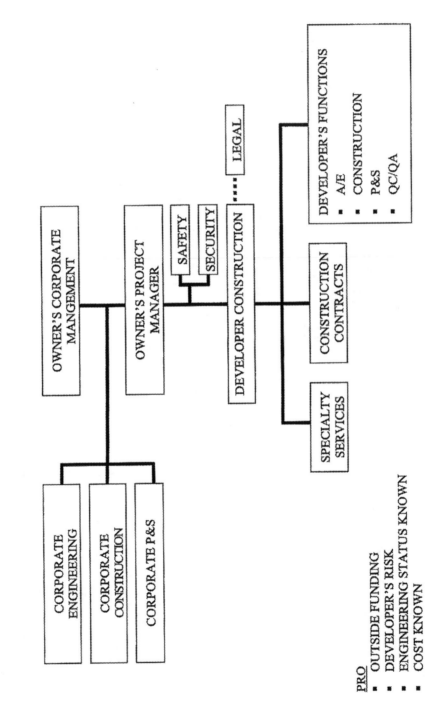

148

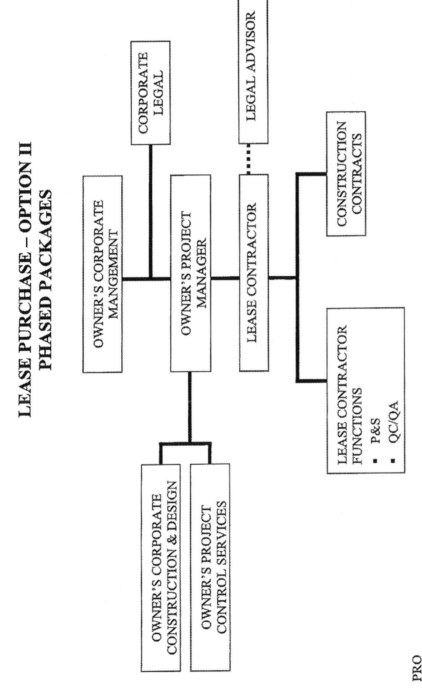

LEASE PURCHASE – OPTION II PHASED PACKAGES

CORPORATE LEGAL

LEGAL ADVISOR

OWNER'S CORPORATE MANGEMENT

OWNER'S PROJECT MANAGER

LEASE CONTRACTOR

CONSTRUCTION CONTRACTS

OWNER'S CORPORATE CONSTRUCTION & DESIGN

OWNER'S PROJECT CONTROL SERVICES

LEASE CONTRACTOR FUNCTIONS
- P&S
- QC/QA

PRO
- FINANANCING NOT UTILITY
- COST KNOWN
- CAN MEET TIGHT SCHEDULE

CON
- CONTRACT PACKAGES NEED TO BE 100%
- UTILITY NEEDS TO FUNCTION
- FAST
- TIMELY EXECUTION

FIGURE #45

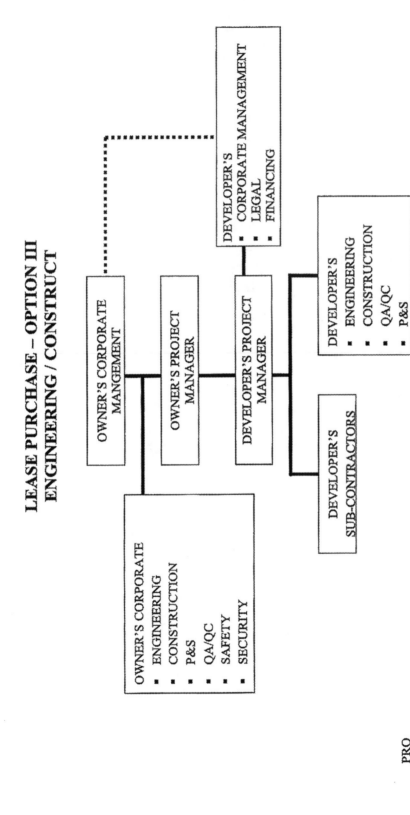

LEASE PURCHASE – OPTION III
ENGINEERING / CONSTRUCT

FIGURE #46

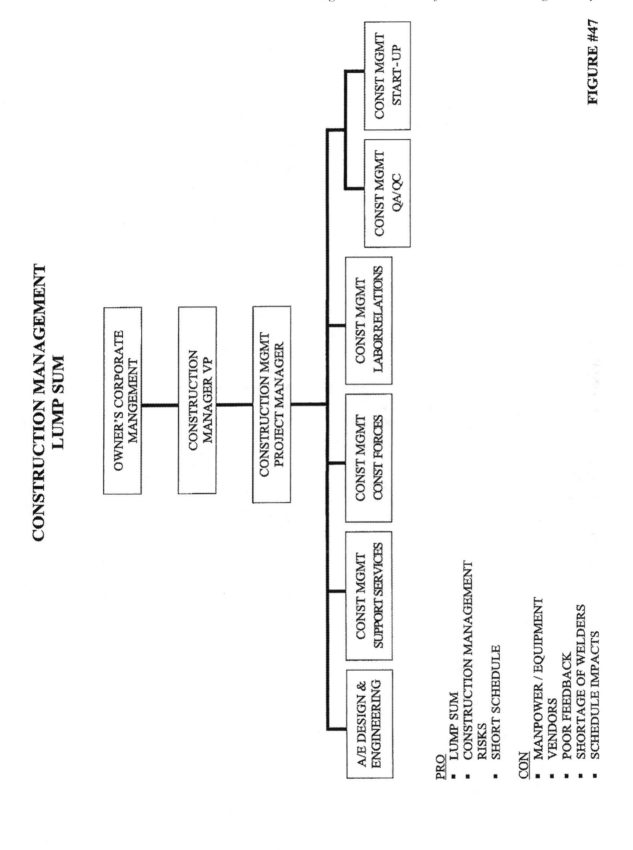

CONSTRUCTION MANAGEMENT LUMP SUM

OWNER'S CORPORATE MANGEMENT

CONSTRUCTION MANAGER VP

CONSTRUCTION MGMT PROJECT MANAGER

A/E DESIGN & ENGINEERING

CONST MGMT SUPPORT SERVICES

CONST MGMT CONST FORCES

CONST MGMT LABOR RELATIONS

CONST MGMT QA/QC

CONST MGMT START-UP

PRO
- LUMP SUM
- CONSTRUCTION MANAGEMENT
- RISKS
- SHORT SCHEDULE

CON
- MANPOWER / EQUIPMENT
- VENDORS
- POOR FEEDBACK
- SHORTAGE OF WELDERS
- SCHEDULE IMPACTS

FIGURE #47

Robert E. Bartz

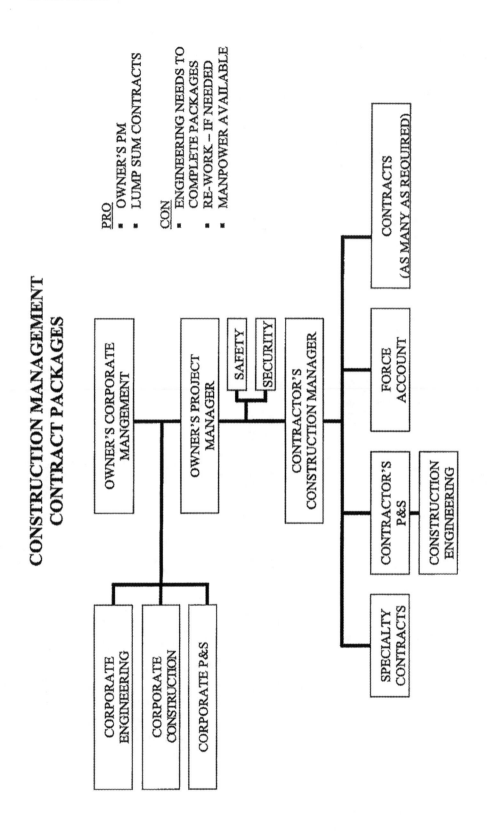

CONSTRUCTION MANAGEMENT
CONTRACT PACKAGES

OWNER'S CORPORATE MANGEMENT

OWNER'S PROJECT MANAGER

SAFETY

SECURITY

CONTRACTOR'S CONSTRUCTION MANAGER

CORPORATE ENGINEERING

CORPORATE CONSTRUCTION

CORPORATE P&S

SPECIALTY CONTRACTS

CONTRACTOR'S P&S

CONSTRUCTION ENGINEERING

FORCE ACCOUNT

CONTRACTS (AS MANY AS REQUIRED)

PRO
- OWNER'S PM
- LUMP SUM CONTRACTS

CON
- ENGINEERING NEEDS TO COMPLETE PACKAGES
- RE-WORK – IF NEEDED
- MANPOWER AVAILABLE

FIGURE #48

152

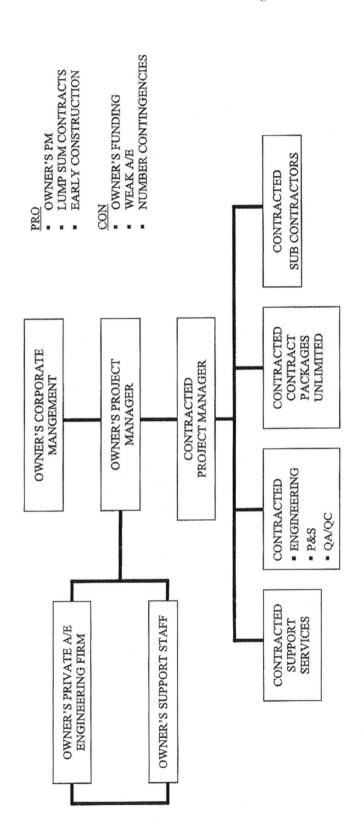

PROJECT MANAGEMENT

Design & Construction of the Contract Package Concept

FIGURE #49

PRO
* OWNER'S PM
* LUMP SUM CONTRACTS
* EARLY CONSTRUCTION

CON
* OWNER'S FUNDING
* WEAK A/E
* NUMBER CONTINGENCIES

OWNER'S CORPORATE MANGEMENT

OWNER'S PROJECT MANAGER

CONTRACTED PROJECT MANAGER

OWNER'S PRIVATE A/E ENGINEERING FIRM

OWNER'S SUPPORT STAFF

CONTRACTED SUB CONTRACTORS

CONTRACTED CONTRACT PACKAGES UNLIMITED

CONTRACTED ENGINEERING
* P&S
* QA/QC

CONTRACTED SUPPORT SERVICES

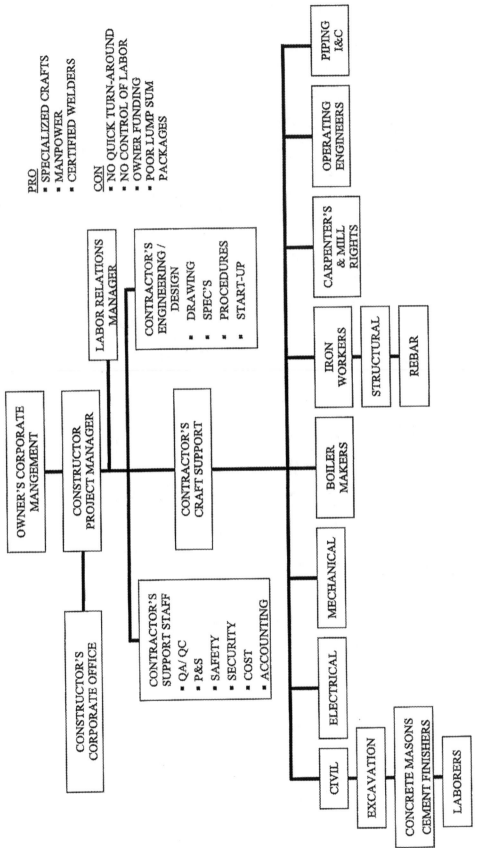

MULTIPLE PACKAGES (BUILDING TRADES)

PRO
- SPECIALIZED CRAFTS
- MANPOWER
- CERTIFIED WELDERS

CON
- NO QUICK TURN-AROUND
- NO CONTROL OF LABOR
- OWNER FUNDING
- POOR LUMP SUM PACKAGES

FIGURE #50

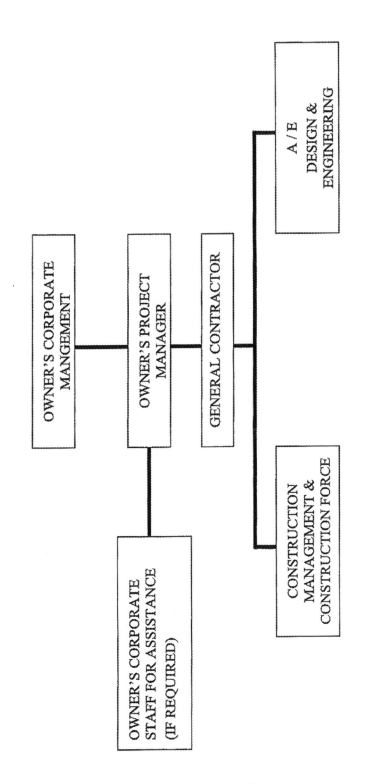

TURN KEY CONTRACT

FIGURE #51

OWNER'S CORPORATE MANGEMENT

OWNER'S PROJECT MANAGER

GENERAL CONTRACTOR

A / E DESIGN & ENGINEERING

OWNER'S CORPORATE STAFF FOR ASSISTANCE (IF REQUIRED)

CONSTRUCTION MANAGEMENT & CONSTRUCTION FORCE

KEY ISSUES
1. LACK OF OWNER INPUT INTO DESIGN
2. POOR COST CONTROL
3. POOR QUALITY OF CONTRACT DOCUMENTS
4. POOR PLANNING / SCHEDULING UPDATES
5. QUALITY WORKMANSHIP
6. POOR CONTRACT LANGUAGE
7. POOR RISK ALLOCATION NOT WELL DEFINED

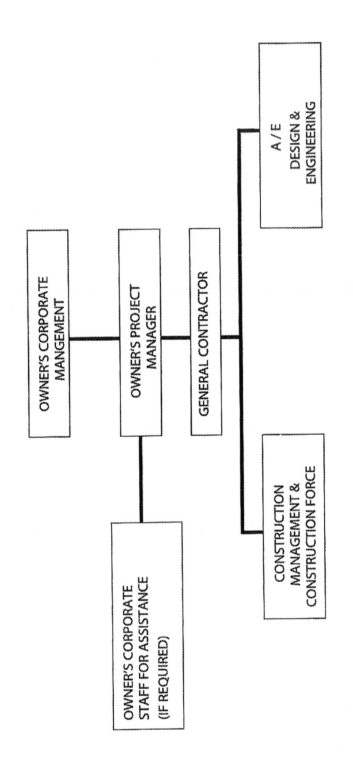

FAST-TRACK

FIGURE #52

KEY ISSUES
1. SIMPLE DESIGN
2. STANDARDIZATION
3. SMALL SIZE
4. VENDOR'S M   EETING SCHEDULE
5. ENGINEERING 3-6 MONTHS LEAD TIME
6. ONE GENERAL CONTRACTOR
7. SITE LIMITATIONS
8. RISK NEW TECHNOLOGY

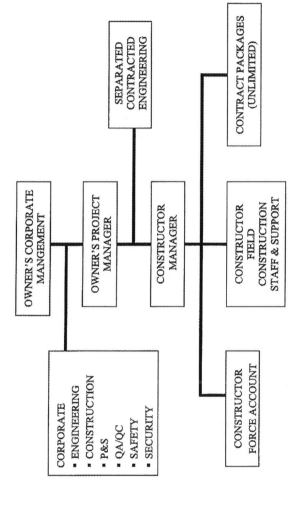

CONSTRUCTION MANAGEMENT WITH CONTRACT PACKAGES & FORCE ACCOUNT

OWNER'S CORPORATE MANGEMENT

OWNER'S PROJECT MANAGER

SEPARATED CONTRACTED ENGINEERING

CONSTRUCTOR MANAGER

CORPORATE
- ENGINEERING
- CONSTRUCTION
- P&S
- QA/QC
- SAFETY
- SECURITY

CONSTRUCTOR FIELD CONSTRUCTION STAFF & SUPPORT

CONTRACT PACKAGES (UNLIMITED)

CONSTRUCTOR FORCE ACCOUNT

PRO
- OWNER'S PROJECT MANAGER
- LUMP SUM CONTRACTS
- ENGINEERING IMPACT
- OWNER'S CONTRACTED ENGINEERING

CON
- TIMELY ENGINEERING PACKAGES
- VENDOR'S MEET NEED DATES
- MANPOWER
- SHORTAGE OF SPECIALIZED CRAFT

FIGURE #53

157

Peculiar Highlights

Each contract denotes an agreement between the Owner and Contractor to handle a particular scope of work. It must be noted that every construction site is unique and has its own peculiar highlights, such as:

Location
Access
County, City, State and Federals Laws
Topography
Surface
Sub surface
Manpower Availability
Transportation
Electricity
Water
Surveys
Freight Facilities
Protection of Site
Fence
Lights
Security
The owner should be aware that enclosed data must be submitted correctly. If data is not submitted correctly, it could result in a claim situation, such as:
General Condition Changes
Supplement Condition Changes
Permits
Site Regulations
Interaction of Federal/State Agencies
Altered Site Conditions
Defective/Deficient Contract Documents
Breach of Contract
Suspensions
Acceleration
Termination
Direct change
Construction Changes
Implied Warranty
Delays
Impossibility of Performance
Weather
Strikes
Owner Purchased Equipment
Maladministration
Licensing Requirements
Liens/Gratis

Safety
Failure to Provide Access to Site
Failure to Review Owner's Ship Drawings
Failure to Provide Timely Inspections
Interference with Contractor's Labor Force
Failure of Progress Payments

Contractor's Responsibility

In selecting a contractor, key issues need to be addressed such as:
The Contractor must be thoroughly familiar with all project requirements.
Contractor must be capable of meeting the Owner's schedule on time and within the budget.
Contractor must visit the job site.
Contractor must have the financial capability.
Contractor must know the pros and cons connected with the performance of work.
Contractor must have experience in hard money contracts.

Contractor understands the general conditions and special conditions.
Contractor is qualified.
Contractor must comply with established procedures.
Contractor must have daily communication to avoid ambiguity and misunderstanding.
All contractor's terms and conditions should be free of vague and unclear statements so assigned work can be completed.
Contractor must keep owner well advised and well informed of all project developments.
Extra work orders and change notices must be handled in timely and orderly manner.

Architect Engineer's Responsibility.

Engineering design work and purchased materials must be available when needed to support construction.
Engineering must control cost overrun and schedule delay for design.
The A/E interprets requirements of the contract.
A/E needs to support the milestone dates in contract package.
Assure completeness of drawings and specs for contract packages.
Must introduce pre-design construction and engineering into site selection as well as the conceptual design.
Serious evaluation of Modular Concepts.
In contract packages the A/E must maintain the boundaries of all drawings and specs.
Working system design A/E must note on engineering drawings all tie ins.
Provide on going design review to ensure cost constructability of plant design.
Maintain "no change" policy once drawings are complete.
If design has major impact, should also have construction impact.
Engineer will provide material needed dates.

Hold engineer accountable.

A/E must protect the owner against defects in contract specs, plans in regard to design materials.

A/E makes sure that design is safe and adequate.

Owner's Responsibilities

Define all contract packages listing work to be accomplished.

Develop an integrated schedule which shows start date and completion date.

Establish computer program to address project status versus planned work, work completed.

Provide site manual which lists descriptions and responsibilities on how the project is to operate.

Develop flow charts to designate responsibility and method to accomplish objectives.

Generate the desire of owner, engineering and contractor to work together and form a team.

Track cost and schedule progress.

Manage the contractor per terms and conditions designated in the contract.

Be fair.

Recognize that the owner is the client and A/E serves the owner.

Develop contracts with good format terms and contracting methods.

My intention with this publication is to be of service to an industry which is in need of experience and guidance. It is further intended to be a guide and helping aid for engineers, owners and constructors in building an electrical generation facility in the most economical and beneficial manner. The preface lays out the present day foundation of commencement and a view of needs for the future of electrical power generation facilities.

It is a prime responsibility of construction management to concern itself with all aspects of subcontract work. Close attention must be directed to the procedures involved in selection of the subcontractor, negotiation of claims and adjustments and acceptance of the work for final payment.

Checklist For Subcontract Pre-Award Conference.

Documents

1. Has bidder received all documents and drawings covering his scope of work?
2. General conditions-question any exceptions.
3. Review of special conditions.
4. Specifications-review page by page if warranted.

Experience—Personnel—Equipment

1. Review of bidder's financial condition.
2. Check previous jobs.
3. Review types of previous jobs.
4. Check references of recent customers.
5. Who is responsible for work for bidder? Will he focus on job?
6. Determine top field representative. What is his experience concerning:
   a. Type of job
   b. Methods of operation
   c. Site conditions
   d. Local labor relations

7. What organizational backup is available for top field representative?
8. Does bidder have necessary procurement and expediting procedures and capabilities?
9. Bidder should state all major construction equipment he intends to employ at site.
10. Condition of equipment.
11. Timely availability of this equipment.
12. What does bidder plan to subcontract and to whom? (Owner reserves the right of approval of subcontractors).

Scope

Has bidder included all separate phases of intended scope; visual review of drawings.
Item by item check of quantities.
Interfaces: does bidder understand the conditions at the start and finish of his scope of work (where his work stops and work of others begins).
Review any changes in design, scope or intent since issue of inquiry not covered by addendum.
Reiterate owner's requirements for cleanup program.

Schedule of Work

Has the schedule of work changed since issue of inquiry?
Exceptions to Start and complete dates, are these dates realistic?
Will bidder accept imposed overtime costs to complete per schedule?
Has bidder analyzed velocity of operation in regard to quantities of items to be installed in given time span?
Has bidder considered manpower?
Precisely what are bidder's intentions as to how many of what crafts are required?
Does bidder have a bar chard or schedule of his work? Will he promptly produce one?
Do we have such a schedule for comparison?
Portions of work now, remobilize later. (additional cost?)

Introduction For General Conditions

General conditions define the rights, responsibilities and relationship of parties concerned. They define either directly or indirectly the interrelationship among the several parties concerned with the construction of a project. These conditions are intended to govern and regulate the obligations of the formal contract.

Definitions:

Owner
Engineer
Contractor
Subcontractor
Contract documents (Contract)
Work
Justification
Approvals
Technical direction
Plant site
Commercial operation
Change order
Supplemental agreement
Contract modification
Contract price
Governing body

Introduction For Supplementary Conditions

Supplementary conditions provide a mechanism for modifying or extending provisions of standardized General Conditions to fit the special requirements of specific projects.

General

Project Location
Working Hours
Addresses
Correspondence, reports and notices

Contractor reports

Progress reports
Force and equipment report
Contractor waiver requests
Un priced purchase orders
Purchase order list
Shipping papers
Reporting frequency

Delivery

>   Shipping
>   Transportation modes to plant site
>   Documentation
>   Preparation for shipment
>   Delivery hours

Site elevation and ambient conditions
Contract post award meeting
Commencement, prosecution and completion of work
Conformance with trade practices
Warranties
Payments to contractor
Price adjustment (escalation)
Format of accounts
Liquidation damages
Schedule

>   Contract Schedule
>   Contractor work plan
>   Contract work plan reports
>   Construction site activities

Construction Reports and Coordination

>   Force and equipment reports
>   Construction quantities reports
>   Material and equipment expediting reports
>   Work Coordination

Additional Insurance Requirements for Plant Site

>   Liability Insurance
>   Contractor's loss insurance

Protection of Site and Facilities

>   Protection of Site
>   Protection of Facilities
>   Interruption of Plant Service
>   Environmental Rules

Contractor's Site Personnel

>   Supervisory Personnel
>   Employee Identification

Labor Relations
Labor Dispute Causing Delays

Site Security/Anti-Terrorism Program
Construction Drawings

As-built drawings
Data to be furnished contractor

Testing and Start Up
Certificate of Conformance
Site Material Practice
Receiving

Unloading
Storage
Movement and Relocation
Salvage, Disposal

Operations and Storage Areas
Expediting of Work
Site and Work Practice

Work week, overtime and shift work by contractor
Use of Premises
Owner's use of equipment and preliminary occupancy

Site and Work Conditions

Baselines and grades
Existing Underground Utilities
Site Information

Site Rules and Regulations

Dust or fume control
General clean up and removal of rubbish
Material restrictions
News releases
Cameras
Firearms
Project Rules

Temporary structures within permanent buildings
Use of Roadways
Site Services and Facilities

First Aid
Fire Protection
Portable water
Telephone Service
Construction power
Communications

Heating Facilities and Ventilation
Hoisting Facilities
Safeguards in Construction

These guidelines will vary, of course, in application to individual projects, but they serve to identify potential trouble areas and thus minimize our exposure to future claims and/or labor problems.

It is essential that the Construction Manager be present at all pre-award interviews with prospective subcontractors. General conditions and supplementary conditions are written guidelines for both owner and contractor to use to describe their contractual obligations.

CHAPTER 6

SUMMARY/CONCLUSION

The theme of this book is to assist A/E Firms, Contractors and Utility owners to obtain the knowledge of how the Contract Package Concept can be developed and implemented for any type or size of project.

The primary motivation for the use of the Contract Package Concept is to divide the job info proper and efficient size packages in order to bid and award the project on a lump sum basis.

In constructing a project of any size or magnitude, it does not require a unique method of management. In managing these activities, construction management must be concerned with the manner and method of how to construct this facility in the most economical and beneficial manner.

This book allows the owner to define his purpose by emphasizing the importance of focus and clarity which in time will assist the Project Organization to zero in on the vision to build a facility on schedule or ahead of schedule and within the budget or under the budget. Management problems affecting the Contract Package are summarized in the following groups:

1. Work Force Problems
2. Contractual Problems
3. Regulatory Problems
4. Design Problems

The area of management expertise has been dormant for the past two decades. It is essential to re-train both new and existing personnel to classify the steps that will help the organization develop and sustain a passion for excellence through ability to convert goals and aspirations into tangible results. Decade by decade, construction concepts become obsolete. Unless the basic concepts on which items are constructed, and clearly understood and explicitly expressed, the contract concept is at the mercy of events. Only a clear definition of the Contract Concept must be clear and realistic to be successful. It is the foundation for priorities, strategies, plans and work assignments.

The Contractor and the Utility needs to review manpower capabilities. Wholesale retirements of experienced personnel reduces a company's technical capabilities and know how and many skilled positions require years of training and experience for a worker to become proficient. In the current economy, cost reductions have reduced spending on recruitment. In many utilities, a comprehensive succession strategy has not been developed for future projects.

There are several critical keys that make this book valuable to the reader.

1. To understand how work can best be planned, scheduled and controlled in a project environment.
2. To understand how to structure work to ensure no communication breakdown will occur, either in-house project member as well as between the customer and contractor.
3. To understand how projects are organized and how organizations function.
4. To understand the working relationships that must exist between the in-house project members as well as between the customer and contractor, regardless of whether they be industrial, government or military personnel, and how the corresponding program offices should interface.

Once the type of project to be built is determined, the owner will develop a tentative list of contract packages which the owner may anticipate for use. This process helps the owner evaluate the status of engineering, procurement, etc. which in turn allows the owner to finalize how the segments of the project will be built by Force Account or Contract Package.

There are five (5) related issues that need to be addressed.

1. Time extensions
2. Who is responsible for the use of contract times?
3. What if the Contract time is too short?
4. What if the Contract time is too long?
5. Who is responsible for the use of Contract time?

This book also contains special features which allows the owner to build a powerful team through open communications, creative innovation and honest evaluation. The Planning Phase of the Contract Package Concept explains the nine (9) major steps in the Management Function.

Objective
Scope
Schedule
Budget
Forecast
Organization
Policy
Procedure
Standard

Planning must occur at every level. The Project Critical Path Schedule can be broken down by area, discipline, budget, etc. the Project Critical Path and Schedule is the story or cook book in the process or method used in determining what the start date and finish date will be. It explains how each activity or milestone is accomplished and how it is to be accomplished. It is imperative for management to understand what the mission is and must

167

convey that understanding to the Project Manager and his team. Having established mission segments and processes allows the project team and management to move forward with a common direction.

There are several benefits to this informative book.

1. The Contract Package Concept provides all types of organizations with the important skills that are needed to build a project in the most beneficial and economical manner.
2. The Contract Package defines the purpose by emphasizing the importance of focus and scope to all parties. It assists organization to zero in on its vision to maintain a schedule of activities allowing the owner to accelerate or slow down the project.
3. The Contract Package Concept will provide the personnel with the important skills needed to build a project and perform and sustain success in building any and all types of projects.
4. The Contract Package Concept is the conscious decision by a team of individuals or organization to achieve something far more productive, profitable and rewarding. It provides the experience, information and know how to build a project on time and within the budget.
5. the Contract Package Concept defines the purpose or vision by emphasizing the importance in which the Contact Package Concept will assist in learning how to gain and sustain the edge in building a successful project.

This book is versatile in its field, in the office or as a reference book. It can be utilized to verify consistency between contract special and general conditions. It can assure that a schedule incorporated in the contract interfaces accurately with the overall project schedule and budget. It can be used to verify that the drawings and specifications are complete for the defined scope of work.

CONCLUSION

In conclusion, this book allows diversification of the manner and method in which any project can be built in the most economical and beneficial manner. This method can be applied in developing residential, commercial, industrial and Power/Energy projects. The price range can accommodate a project in any amount from one hundred dollars to over one billion dollars plus.

At this time in our history, the United States is in a quagmire. Our current energy sources are aging rapidly. Today our state governments are establishing and directing what type of power plants should be allowed to be built in their state. It should be noted that construction permits for nuclear power stations have risen to the top of acceptable power sources. Our federal and state governments must finalize the requirements to the type of fuel, environmental issues, technologies that will be allowed.

Time is of the essence! With the price of fuel climbing rapidly and the value of the U.S. dollar in decline, the rise of commercial items and products, we must be able to expect the unexpected and be prepared for it. Federal and state governments, utilities, A/E firms and contractors are all in a precarious situation. They realize that certain criteria will need to be improved rapidly, such as

1. Political Leadership
2. State/Federal Review Boards
3. Licensing
4. Manufacturing Capabilities
5. Vendor Capabilities
6. Engineering Experience
7. Building Crafts and Manpower
8. Management
9. Utility Operations
10. Retired Work Source
11. Standardized Design
12. Training

Whatever the final decision to resolve the energy needs, it will be accomplished by selecting the type of project and the manner and methods required to construct it. The resolution should include the follow key issues:

Organization
Architect/Engineer
Management
Integrated Schedule
Summary

ORGANIZATION

Whatever type of organization a company may adapt, it is imperative that management decisions, direction and practices play an important roll for success. Some of the highlights which have affected various projects are because the Owner's Organization of those projects declined to do the following:

1. Delegate adequate authority and responsibility for project management terms.
2. Construction and erection schedules were established and did not integrate engineering procurement and construction.
3. Failed to effectively manage Construction Contractors to the terms and conditions of the specific contract.
4. Failure to hold A/E accountable to terms and conditions of their contract. The Owner is the client and the A/E serves the Owner, not the Owner serving the A/E.
5. Develop contracts with good formats, contractual terms or contracting methods.

6. The Project Management Team must establish a system which inter relates cost and schedule on a current and factful basis.

It is only common sense that if a decision to divide the construction work into many relatively small contract packages and the Organization fails to adequately manage them, it can significantly contribute to schedule and cost problems

The object of directing or developing Construction Contract Format and terms is to get the Owner, Contractor and Engineer to work towards the same objective which is the earliest achievable completion date and the lowest possible cost.

We must realize that if we fail to manage the numerous Contractors will only result in a series of conflicts of contractual obligations. The Contractors are scheduled to meet scheduled milestones by a given date, but performance is not possible if the Contractor work area is occupied by another Contractor, or Owner material is missing or design problems.

ARCHITECT ENGINEERS.

Many times the Owners disregard the contract terms; the required Contractors submittals, design, and contractual obligations and scheduled duration for performance have been ignored.

Owners need to adapt a professional attitude or stance and ensure that the Architect Engineer performs in accordance with the contractual obligations. In the same means, the Owner must fulfill its contractual obligations in a timely and orderly manner. The Owner should not dilute the Architect Engineer's responsibility for design.

In order to efficiently carry on a complex construction project, engineering design work and purchased materials must be available when needed to support construction.

Engineering and procurement schedules must be coordinated and tied with the construction schedule so that they can be adjusted to coincide with any change in sequence of construction.

The Architect Engineer can significantly contribute to the cost overrun and schedule delays if not held in check.

The Owners integrated organization must see that procurement and design are not hindered or slowed down. They must not interfere with material and engineering support for construction or contribute to unnecessary rework; avoid access and interference on the jobsite and avoid disrupting inspection activities. Do not forget the main goal is to "build the project". We have a schedule and a budget, there will be changes and changed conditions. Try to expect the unexpected, the flexible, and pre plat-manage the project.

The Owner's Organization must instantly develop the ability to produce timely, relevant, decisive direction and resolutions. They must also abstain and make sure that ambiguity of specific definitions of responsibility and authority.

The Owner's upper management or corporate home office must give to project level management the authority to carry out their responsibilities. Stringent approval requirements and if all decisions at project level are reviewed and approved by the Owner's upper management this will lead to frustrating and demoralizing affects. It must also be noted burdensome bureaucratic procedures can produce inefficiencies. The procedures and inefficiencies can be time consuming, and seriously impact decision making process.

If delegated authority is not given so the organization team members have the ability to deal with the A/E, and contractors effectively, the project could be heading for failure.

INTEGRATED SCHEDULE.

Next to authority, the organization must have the ability to tract cost and schedule progress at the detailed level, as well as to accurately predict the cost and schedule implications of proposed changes. Lacking such a system it is extremely difficult for management to achieve effective accountability. The need to incorporate the budget and schedules is important because it allows management to:

1. Measure progress in an objective and detailed manner and method in which level of work is performed.
2. Quickly identify problems.
3. Assess the costs or schedule delays.

Lack of an integrated schedule seriously hinders long term planning and coordination of procurement, engineering and construction. This in turn results in immediate problems and contractor access, contractor interference, lack of timely materials and engineering to support construction and impaired management visibility and flexibility. The lack of an integrated schedule also affects contractor performance. Work packages are not produced in a complete and timely manner.

Scheduling problems have idled constructors and caused conditions to deviate from bid specifications removing the Owner's legal basis to resist contractor's claims and resultant change orders.

In closing, the most important ingredients for a successful organization are:

1. Have an organization with defined responsibility and authority.
2. The organization needs management's direction and objectives and Charter in Life.
3. Enforce contracts-be fair.
4. Ability and capability to take care of business

It is mandatory to verify that the overall approach of the contract package is consistent with the project approach. It requires a check of the scope, method of building etc. Construct a plan that will help successfully navigate by expecting the unexpected and be prepared to make a prudent management decision in a timely and orderly manner and avoid or minimize the impact on budget and schedule.

The book is versatile in its use in the field, office or as a reference book. It can be utilized to verify consistency between contract special general conditions. It can assure that the schedule incorporated in the contract interfaces accurately with the overall project schedule and budget. It can be used to verify the drawings and specifications are complete for the defined scope of work.

The key benefits of the Contract Package Concept are:

1. The Contract Package Concept provides all types of organizations with the important skills that are needed to build a project in the most beneficial and economical manner.
2. The Contract Package Concept defines the purpose by emphasizing the importance of focus and scope. It assists organizations "zero in" on its vision.
3. The Contract Package Concept will provide the individual or organization with the important skills they need to build a project and perform and sustain success in building any and all types of projects.
4. The Contract Package Concept is the conscious decision by a team of individuals or organization to achieve something far more productive, profitable and rewarding. It provides the experience, information and "know how" to build a project on time and within the budget.
5. The Contract Package Concept defines the purpose or vision by emphasizing the importance in which the Contract Package Concept will assist in learning how to gain and sustain the edge in building a successful project.

There are several critical keys that make this book valuable to the reader. Some of them are:

1. To understand how work can best be planned, scheduled and controlled in a project environment.
2. To understand how to structure work so that no communications breakdown will occur either in house or between the customer and contractor.
3. To understand how projects are organized and how organizations function.
4. To understand the working relationships that must exist between the in house project member as well as between the customer and contractor, regardless of whether they be industrial, government or military personnel, and how the corresponding program offices should interface.

The Contract Package Concept consists of a series of layers of decision and conclusions, moving from the general to the specific. Each decision preparing the way for the next. The final plan naturally emerges as the result of the successful completion of all the proceeding steps. The Contract Package Concept format is essential to focus first on particular needs and wants then designs the strategies for the format that will satisfy those needs and wants. Goals become targets or milestones of reference for measuring progress.

The Contract Package Concept would appeal to the following countries or regions: North America, South America, European Market, Eastern Caribbean and parts of the Far East.

There are certain limitations in using the Contract Package Concept. They are:

Scope-understanding what is needed.
Size-many countries need large projects, but lack experience.
Language-Certain terms and issues have alternate meanings.
Money-various values and amounts result in financial limitations.
Contract terms and Conditions-result in misunderstanding or just don't exist.
Consultants-some countries can't pay for them.

Procrastination is the true death to any Owner's Construction Project and Organization if the ability to manage is missing. If we do not have a well defined scope, the next steps we hear are budget and scheduling problems, contractor delays and claims and design problems.

ABOUT THE AUTHOR

Robert Bartz has over 35 years experience in the area of project/construction management for domestic and international projects. He is an experienced manager, highly knowledgeable in all phases of project management, project development, business administration, business development, construction management, contract development, contract administration and contract package concept. He is the owner and CEO of a construction/management company and has experience in providing contract administration for the following countries following the Gulf War: Kuwait, Yemen, Egypt and Jordan. He has reviewed and developed studies for 500 KV transmission line for Belize, Honduras and Costa Rica. He served as Director of new projects and served as a Consultant for the Southeast Region of the United States. He served as Project General Manager for Fossil Projects:

Energy Capacity Studies, Projects for future generation/technology
New Generation-850 M Combined Cycle for Martin County, FL
Re-powering of 420 MW oil fired fossil power plant
Martin County, FL Reservoir Breach Investigation/Reconstruction
St. Johns River Power Park, Jacksonville, FL, 2-650 MW Coal Fired Fossil Units.
Solar Waste projects
Nuclear review

After his retirement from the largest utility company in Florida, Robert continues to act as a consultant in the construction and management fields.